T
PYRAMID
MIND

THE PYRAMID MIND

The Six-Part Programme for
Complete Happiness and Success

DR VICTOR BLANPSO

SIMON & SCHUSTER

THE
PYRAMID
MIND

The Six-Part Programme for
Confidence, Happiness and Success

DR VLAD BELIAVSKY

SIMON &
SCHUSTER

London · New York · Sydney · Toronto · New Delhi

First published in Great Britain by Simon & Schuster UK Ltd, 2023

1 3 5 7 9 10 8 6 4 2

Simon & Schuster UK Ltd
1st Floor
222 Gray's Inn Road
London WC1X 8HB

www.simonandschuster.co.uk
www.simonandschuster.com.au
www.simonandschuster.co.in

Simon & Schuster Australia, Sydney
Simon & Schuster India, New Delhi

A CIP catalogue record for this book
is available from the British Library

Paperback ISBN: 978-1-3985-0746-3
eBook ISBN: 978-1-3985-0747-0

Typeset in Stone Serif by M Rules
Printed and Bound using 100% Renewable
Electricity at CPI Group (UK) Ltd

MIX
Paper | Supporting
responsible forestry
FSC
www.fsc.org   FSC® C171272

Contents

Part Three

The Bottom Pyramid

Part Four

The Way to Personal Mastery

Appendix

Introduction

In Pursuit of Ultimate Mastery

WHAT TO EXPECT

- In the Introduction, I provide the background information. You will learn, for example, what integrative psychotherapy is, how it is connected to the Pyramid Model, my motivation to write this book, and why I sometimes use combat sport metaphors in this book.

- In Part One, I introduce and explain the Pyramid Model itself. We will get familiar with some scientific concepts and terms that will help us to understand better how the Pyramid Model is organised. We will also delve into cutting-edge psychology and neuroscience, and consider intriguing case studies.

- In Parts Two and Three, I describe how best to work with your mind. Each chapter explains a specific aspect of how you function. They emphasise what holds you back and offer actionable strategies on how to manage and improve yourself. This part of the book is a comprehensive and science-based programme for anyone who wants to develop skills of self-mastery and thus become a healthy, confident, happy and more successful person.

- In Part Four, we will learn how to apply the Pyramid Model in real life and how to develop your self-care skills.

MY STORY:
How it all started

How to make the world a better place? That was the question that bothered me a lot during my teenage years. Maybe that's because I was growing up when Ukraine, my homeland, was going through a significant political and social turbulence. I was still a boy, for example, when I first went to the central square with my friends, skipping the whole day at school, to see how millions of adults took part in the series of national protests.

How to make the world a better place? Maybe I was thinking about this question because I loved history. I could spend the whole night with my father in the kitchen, discussing different time periods, the rise and fall of civilisations, bold reforms that changed how people lived, or the victories and mistakes of different rulers.

Maybe I was just sensitive to the injustices and sufferings of others and wanted the world to be a little bit kinder to those who inhabit it. Or perhaps it was just the age of puberty and hormones that pushed me to rebel against the current state of affairs. I don't know.

More importantly, I also did not understand how to make a difference. Where to start? Shall I go abroad and do some volunteer teaching? Shall I study hard to become a politician and then fight for reforms? Maybe I should try to earn a lot of money and then donate to a good cause? I was not sure which way would be the right one.

Shortly thereafter, I entered a university and started to read very light philosophy from time to time. Perhaps on some level I hoped that the greatest thinkers of all time could give me the answers, or at least the direction in which to search. And it helped.

There was one thought which lots of thinkers seemed to reiterate in different variations. For example, here is how it was expressed by Mahatma Gandhi: 'If you want to change the world, start with yourself.' Here are some other examples of a similar message: 'The world as we have created it is a process of our thinking. It cannot be changed without changing our thinking' – Albert Einstein. 'He who conquers others is strong; he who conquers himself is mighty' – Lao Tzu. 'He who lives in harmony with himself lives in harmony with the world' – Marcus Aurelius. 'Peace comes from within. Don't seek it without' – Buddha.

'Start with yourself.' I am not sure that I actually understood what it meant at that point. But for some reason this thought resonated with me strongly. It stuck deeply in my mind, getting only stronger with time, and occupying more and more of my thoughts and attention.

Perhaps, as a person who loved history, I imagined that what if those great rulers of the past and present 'started with themselves'? What if they knew how to identify and challenge their biases? What if they didn't take their anger and hurt out on others? What if they were at peace with themselves? Maybe, in such scenarios, there would be less war and violence in this world?

I then posed the same question to myself. 'What if I started with myself?' To be honest, I had to admit that I thought a lot about changing the world but hardly ever thought of becoming a better version of myself. But what if I did? What if I knew how to come to grips with myself? What if I found peace of mind as a result?

Of course, I wouldn't be able to stop any wars or cruelty on the planet. But perhaps, if I lived in harmony with myself, I would be disposed to create and maintain harmony around myself? In my family ... in friends ... at work ... in my neighbourhood. *That's a good beginning*, I thought.

MY JOURNEY:
The search for the right tool

The goal was set. It was now clear where I wanted to come. It felt quite exciting and relieving at the same time. But now I needed a plan how to reach the destination. Frustratingly, there were many of those who were saying that it would be great to have mastery of yourself, but nobody seemed to give a concise and practical instruction of how to actually do it. I remember reading this phrase, 'He who lives in harmony with himself lives in harmony with the world', by Marcus

Aurelius, over and over again, and then I kind of responded: 'Okay, Marcus, I got you. I agree totally, but how?'

I've always felt that life would be much easier if it came with some sort of a mind instruction manual. The mind determines everything we do, how we think and how we feel from the moment we are born, but most of us have practically no idea how it works and how to manage it.

It is like driving a car. Without a car owner's manual, we have no clue what the dashboard lights mean. If nobody explained it to you, you wouldn't know how to operate the controls or how to respond to the actions of others safely. And if nobody told you that an engine needs oil to function, you wouldn't think about changing the oil – until your car stops dead in the middle of the road.

So, where to start? My decision was to study psychology, psychotherapy and philosophy. After all, it is those disciplines that are primarily concerned with the question of how our mind is organised and how to achieve inner mastery. But it was not the whole package. On top of that, at that time, I was also practising martial arts with great enthusiasm.

You may wonder what on earth combat sport has to do with the idea of achieving inner peace and living in harmony with the world. It looks to be the direct opposite of those. Frankly speaking, combat sport was just a part of my fitness routine at that time. I've been into sports since my early childhood and liked all kinds of physical activity.

It wasn't the fight itself that I liked in combat sport. For example, I did not fight in the streets to prove any dominance over others. Nor did I enter major competitions to win any big titles. The only person who seemed to suffer from my sport was my younger brother, Paul. For example, there was a period when I was actively training in aikido. Once I had learned a new technique, like some kind of wrist hold, for example, I wanted to practise it as often as possible to improve my skills. And as you might have guessed, I often came to my poor bro with this intention. Paul was very excited at first, as he was also learning some cool stuff with me, which he could then show to his friends at school. But after a few months or so, he started to run away from me for some reason. I suppose my moves were not as smooth as I thought ... sorry brother. But at least you still know how to do a perfect kotegaeshi.*

It was not about the fight itself. I enjoyed, first and foremost, that martial arts training involved many physical benefits, such as improved fitness, self-defence and endurance. However, with time, I began to notice that the training also led to some mental benefits. Many of those who came to the gym seemed to change over time. Those who came hurt or vulnerable became gradually much more confident and resilient. Many of those who came aggressive or hostile became a little bit calmer and self-disciplined. Most of the black belts I knew, not to mention grand masters, were highly cool and friendly people who would do everything to avoid any real fight in the street.

So, I suppose martial arts training is probably another way you can achieve some kind of personal mastery and even peace with yourself and others. Of course, it is not always the case. And it differs from what psychotherapy or

---

* Kotegaeshi (wrist twist or wrist turn-out) is a popular throwing technique in aikido, which involves twisting an attacker's wrist.

philosophy can offer. Yet it does not conflict with them, and actually all those things can be complementary. You can train both your mind and body at the same time, can't you?

In fact, for this reason, many philosophers of the past were also athletes. Did you know, for example, that Plato was a fighter? Plato was well known for his physique* and was particularly skilled at wrestling. He excelled so much that he reportedly participated at the Isthmian Games (comparable to the Olympics).

Okay, that's all for the background. Now, we can finally come to the point of this story. Though martial arts and psychotherapy may seem to be from different planets, there was one thing that they seemed to have in common. At least, I've noticed over time that I tend to show the same attitude or the same approach while training and practising in both of those fields. It turned out that it was really hard for me to stay within the boundaries of just one school, whether it was a school of psychotherapy or of martial arts. Don't get me wrong, it is not that I lacked focus or commitment. I never quit or gave up once enrolled in the course. I always diligently followed the curriculum and mastered everything that my tutors or coaches could teach me. But it never felt enough. That was the problem. Every spare moment, on weekends, for example, I would always go and learn some

---

* Plato's given name was actually Aristocles, after his grandfather. But his wrestling coach dubbed him 'Platon' once, which means 'broad', on account of his broad-shouldered figure. The nickname Plato just stuck.

other things elsewhere. Sometimes it felt that I was 'cheating' on my tutors.

Let's get back to the aikido example. Did you know that there are many different schools of aikido? There are actually more than fifteen styles.* Personally, back then, I was learning the so-called Yoshinkan aikido, which is known as a 'hard' or practical style. This is one of the styles that has been taught to the Tokyo police, for example. Anyway, we had a really skilled sensei, the holder of the highest rank in the country, and the training itself was great. But what I could not understand was why we ignored some interesting techniques that were taught in other aikido schools across the street.

Here is an example. At some point, I was obsessed with joint-lock techniques.† It was explained to us, in our dojo, that if someone grabs your wrist, for example, you can do, let's say, A, B and C to defend yourself. And these were effective techniques, no doubt. But then I looked around and explored what other aikido styles were teaching. And it turned out that there were also D, E and F options. After that, I looked around again and checked what other schools of martial arts were doing, such as hapkido, Brazilian jujitsu, judo and so on. And it turned out that there was a wide range of other possibilities. As I was doing my research, in some sense it felt that I was collecting the alphabet.

---

* Those schools were founded by direct students of Morihei Ueshiba, the founder of aikido.

† A joint lock is a grappling technique, which involves manipulation of an opponent's joints. It can involve twisting, pulling, pushing or bending fingers, wrists, ankles, etc. in an 'unnatural' direction.

'Why would you do that?' you may ask. I just felt that if you had multiple options, if you had a diverse skill set, you would be better prepared for a fight. If some technique does not work for some reason, you can quickly switch to something else. If someone grabs your hand, for example, you can try to rotate your opponent's arm one way. If he or she resists, you can rotate it the other way. If it still does not work, you can grab and twist their pinkie, and so on.

Believe it or not, I experienced the exact same thing in my therapeutic training. It was really hard for me to ignore other therapeutic approaches. For example, I've always been a big fan of CBT (cognitive behavioural therapy). I like so many things about it: it is short-term, very precise and supported by tons of empirical research. It is almost perfect. But guess what? Yes, I've looked around. I was simply very curious what other schools of thought could offer. And it proved that there was a variety of things.

At some point I discovered, for example, mindfulness-based interventions. With CBT, for instance, you learn to recognise and challenge your negative thoughts, analysing their logic, identifying fallacies in your conclusions, considering alternative points of view, and so forth. By contrast, with mindfulness-based interventions, you are encouraged to pay attention to your thoughts and feelings in a non-judgemental manner (without placing judgements on what you think or feel). These two approaches are quite different in nature. But nonetheless, the important point is that, according to studies, both methods can be very effective for treatment or self-care. So, why would we ignore one of those methods then, I asked myself repeatedly.

I also liked something about the psychodynamic approach. CBT and mindfulness-based therapies are basically 'present moment' therapies. That means they seek to solve a problem that you have here and now. But they don't really care much about how or why you happen to have this problem. For example, if you think badly of yourself, those therapies will help you to cope with your negative thinking. But usually, they won't guide you to understand why you started to think badly of yourself in the first place. Sometimes it is totally fine. But sometimes you may want to dig a little bit deeper and identify the causes or the origin of your problems. For example, one person may want to understand why she started to think, let's say, 'I am unattractive.' Some other person may want to figure out of why he began to believe that it is bad to show feelings of love and attachment. That's where psychodynamic therapy can be of use. The psychodynamic approach pays lots of attention to our past. It seeks to understand, in particular, how our past experiences (relationships with our parents, partners or other significant figures) shaped who we are today.

I definitely did not like that psychodynamic therapy could literally take years. It looked sometimes like digging for the sake of digging. But the idea itself made perfect sense. If you manage to understand where a problem came from, it would be easier for you to prevent this problem from recurring in the future. For instance, a person with the belief *I'm unattractive* may recognise that the reason why she came to hold this thought is because her mother used to compare her a lot with other girls. With this in mind, this person may both let go of this self-sabotaging belief and adopt a different style of behaviour towards others, treating her own children, for example, with much more unconditional love.

To sum up, it was really hard for me to stay within the boundaries of just one approach. I could not help but look beyond those boundaries again and again. It just felt that you could always find something interesting, valuable or really unique over there. So I kept looking.

Importantly, at some point I realised that many of those cool things found in different places could actually be combined. After a closer look, it turned out that many methods of different schools are complementary and could go well together. For example, why not use techniques from CBT and mindfulness-based interventions together? And, if there is a need, why not also resort to some techniques from the psychodynamic approach? You can apply just one method if it works well for you or meets the needs of your clients, no doubt. But if it doesn't work well enough, or if it is not sufficient, you could have an arsenal of other tools at your disposal.

It should be noted that I was not the first person to think about this possibility. One day I was surprised to discover that in martial arts there was already the so-called MMA (mixed martial arts), which was still quite a marginal sport when I first heard about it. Meanwhile, it turned out that in psychotherapy there was the so-called integrative therapy, which again was not very well known in my environment when I first came across it.

Frankly speaking, it was a great relief to find like-minded people. I could finally stop feeling that I was 'cheating' on my teachers by attending the workshops of other masters. It was 'legal' to look around as much as you wanted to. You could learn from anyone, broaden your outlook, diversify your skill set, and even develop any brand-new things (e.g. theories, frameworks for treatment or self-development, styles of fight, etc.).

Below, I will give more details about integrative therapy and MMA. It will be a short overview of how those two approaches came into being, and why it became popular to mix things together. Maybe I am too biased, and those two fields just became too intertwined in my head over the years, but I've always felt that there are many fascinating parallels between integrative therapy and MMA.

Let me clarify one point here, though, before we go any further. I mention MMA just because it is a good metaphor to understand one of the main themes of this book. It is not a story about being tough, competitive or becoming a fighter. It is the exact opposite. It is a story about respect for others, the value of co-operation and importance of being open-minded. It is a story about how you can develop extraordinary mastery in your field by being willing to learn from those who come from different backgrounds.

FROM 'HUMAN COCKFIGHTING' TO MMA

When it comes to combat sport, there is always the age-old question: 'What is the best martial art?' Every martial artist has had this question asked many times by friends, fellow fighters or newcomers who want to expand their knowledge in the field. Who would win in a fight: a boxer or a karate black belt? Can a wrestler beat a kickboxer? How about: Bruce Lee vs Muhammad Ali?

In 1993, Rorion Gracie, a jujitsu practitioner, along with businessmen Art Davie and John Milius, set out to settle this long-argued debate once and for all. Together they decided to start a tournament that would feature the best fighters who had very different combat styles. The tournament was called the Ultimate Fighting Championship (UFC). The goal of UFC was to answer that popular sports fans' question: What is the best martial art in the world?

The organisers invited the fighters to face off – to have a full-contact, no-holds-barred contest – to determine who reigned supreme. And the challenge was accepted.

The very first tournament (UFC 1) was held on 12 November 1993 in Denver, Colorado, with a $50,000 prize for the winner. The event featured eight fighters from different martial arts backgrounds, such as savate, sumo, kickboxing, American kenpo karate, Brazilian jujitsu, boxing, shootfighting and taekwondo. The fighters were pitted against one another – so a boxer against a sumo wrestler; kickboxer against karateka. It was a one-day, single-elimination tournament where the winner of a fight progressed to the next round. The champion was the one who won all their fights that night.

The tournament was won by Royce Gracie, a Brazilian jujitsu black belt and younger brother of Rorion Gracie, co-founder of UFC. The two brothers were members of the renowned Gracie fighting family, who had founded Brazilian jujitsu.*

---

* Brazilian jujitsu, also known as Gracie jujitsu, was developed around 1920 by Brazilian brothers Carlos and Helio Gracie.

Just in case you are not a martial arts fan, Brazilian jujitsu is a combat style that is based on grappling and ground fighting. It focuses on taking an opponent down to the ground, wrestling to gain a dominant position, and using various submission techniques (such as joint locks and choke holds) to subdue an opponent.

Originally, Royce Gracie, a skinny guy in a gi* with an unknown fighting style at that time, was generally considered to be an underdog. Most fans and experts expected to see strikers, such as a boxer or a karateka, dominate the competition. Oh, how wrong they were. Shockingly, submission skills proved the most effective during that first big fight night. Royce methodically took three opponents down and forced them to submit in less than five minutes overall.

It is important to note here that in the early days of UFC, there was no such thing as MMA (mixed martial arts), as we know it today. Again, UFC started as a competition that pitted fighters of different styles against one another to test their skills. On the whole, most fighters in the early period were one-dimensional. They were specialists in a particular martial art and tended to have skills just in one discipline, such as boxing, judo and so on.

With time, however, as the founders of UFC put on more and more of these competitions, one thing happened that no one expected. Fighters began to 'borrow' effective techniques from other styles, rather than dogmatically following just one, which gradually led to the development of a separate fighting style known today as mixed martial arts (MMA).

---

* The gi is a uniform for training in Brazilian jujitsu.

Some athletes, for example, soon began to realise that their styles were too restrictive and did not prepare them for all fighting situations. So they had to go and train in other disciplines to be able to defend themselves from the attacks of their opponents.

If we go back to Royce Gracie and the formative years of UFC, Royce dominated the ring because he was a master in ground fighting, while most of his opponents had no idea how to deal with a grappler. They were still great fighters who were successful in their own sport, yet none of them was able to stop Royce from taking them down and forcing them to submit. After Royce dominated the first five UFC tournaments, it became clear that there was a need for his rivals to change their approach.* Many 'stand-up' fighters decided to adapt and learn techniques from Brazilian jujitsu so that they could stop getting beaten by grapplers such as Royce.

Enter cross-training. It was not only jujitsu. Fighters started to take the best moves from different styles in order to develop their strength. Pure strikers began to train in wrestling so that they could defend themselves from takedowns and keep on their feet. Pure wrestlers began to add striking techniques to their arsenal, and then either work for a submission or inflict damage with strikes. Do you know

---

* Royce went on to win the second UFC tournament (UFC 2), defending his champion's title and reasserting the dominance of Brazilian jujitsu. Then he made his way to the final of UFC 3 but ended up withdrawing due to exhaustion and dehydration. After that, he won UFC 4 and fought to a draw in the final of UFC 5.

how 'ground and pound' got started, for example?* It was a tactic originally employed by wrestlers, who combined takedowns and strikes.

Frank Shamrock took training in multiple disciplines to a completely new level. Most of Frank's original training was based in submission wrestling, which meant he had a strong ground game. But later on he decided to learn kickboxing and improve his striking techniques. By the time Frank made his UFC debut in 1997, he was already well versed in grappling, striking and takedowns. Plus, he was perfectly conditioned, having included a great deal of cardio fitness in his training to be able to fight all night if necessary.

And it worked perfectly. In 1997, Shamrock was the first fighter to win the UFC middleweight championship.† After that, he went on to defend his belt four times and retired as an undefeated champion.

Frank was not afraid to adapt and diversify his skill set, which is what gave him the edge. On the one hand, with a mix of skills, Frank became more unpredictable than traditional fighters, which allowed him to catch his opponents off guard. No one knew what would come next. On the other hand, being equally skilled in different aspects of the fight game, Frank was better prepared to exploit the weaknesses of his opponents. For example, he could either toss

---

* 'Ground and pound' is a tactic, primarily used in MMA, in which a competitor takes an opponent to the mat and begins landing strikes from the top position.
† The UFC middleweight championship was later renamed the light heavyweight championship.

a striker to the ground or force a grappler to stand, where those fighters had very little to offer.

From that point forward, athletes from all over the world recognised the need to cross-train to be successful in UFC. It was no longer enough to have a black belt in one martial art. Rather, from now on, it was necessary to become a well-rounded or multi-dimensional fighter, with a diverse set of skills and tactics. Not doing so would simply result in defeat.

Thus, the mixed martial artist was born. UFC, in turn, slightly changed its concept and became one of the organisations that held and promoted MMA bouts.

MMA has also become a sport in its own right. Before MMA was mainstream, fighters trained in different martial arts separately and then intuitively tried to combine the techniques. Today, young fighters can join MMA gyms and study MMA specifically from scratch from experienced coaches.

And there is a lot to learn about. There are technical differences, specific training processes and fight scenarios that are not present in other disciplines. For example, boxers and kickboxers are usually taught to keep their hands up. A high guard is meant to block punches or kicks to the head. By contrast, most MMA fighters would keep their hands rather low. That's because having the hands low makes it easier to defend against takedowns.

If we go back to the formative years of UFC and then watch it over the years, it is easy to see how quickly the sport evolved. Conceptually, it all started with the goal of bringing different martial arts performers together and showcasing their skills. Back then, there were few fighters who could grapple at all, and most of the athletes were one-dimensional. But it gradually progressed to the point where each fighter had a mix of fighting skills.

Today, MMA is often described as the fastest-growing sport in the world. If it keeps going like this, it might soon become the most viewed combat sport worldwide, surpassing the popularity of boxing. To illustrate this, in less than thirty years, UFC grew from a marginal television event to a global phenomenon with a huge fanbase worldwide. In 2016, UFC was sold for a whopping $4 billion, reportedly making it the largest sale in the history of professional sport.

In conclusion, let's return to the question posed at the beginning of this section. What's the best martial art? I suppose the harsh truth that the UFC events revealed was that none of the pure fighting styles had all the answers. No matter how proficient you are in boxing, for example, if you don't have an understanding of how to protect yourself from the deep waters, and you are matched up against someone who is adept at wrestling, you will find yourself smashed on to the floor and end up being forced to submit. Same goes for grapplers. It does not matter how good your Brazilian jujitsu is, if you don't know how to fight standing up, and you are matched up against someone with a good takedown defence and proper striking, you will get knocked out.

Do you see what I am getting at? It is great if you specialise in one discipline. It will certainly help you in a fight. But if you stick to just one skill set, it will only take you so far.

Another option is to let go of the old way, of thinking that your style is the best, and be ready to learn from masters from different backgrounds. In this case, there is no limit to how far you can go.

FROM 'THERAPY WARS' TO INTEGRATIVE PSYCHOTHERAPY

Psychotherapy is only 100 years old but, according to some estimates, there are already more than 400 types of therapy. These can be defined and grouped by theoretical models (psychodynamic, cognitive, humanistic, etc.), format (individual, family, group), length and frequency of sessions (short-term, long-term), methods of work (direct or indirect, with instructions and home assignments or not), techniques used (behavioural experiments, questioning, etc.), kinds of issues addressed (from treating personality disorders to weight-loss problems), and so on.

There are, however, a few main players in the game. Below, I list some common types, schools or directions of psychotherapy. Meanwhile, there are dozens of individual therapies that work under the umbrellas of these schools.

Type of therapy	Description	Examples
Cognitive therapy	Seeks to identify and modify dysfunctional ways of thinking. It primarily examines thoughts and beliefs that may affect a person in a negative way.	– Cognitive behavioural therapy (CBT) – Rational emotive behaviour therapy (REBT)

Type of therapy	Description	Examples
Behavioural therapy	Focuses on changing behaviours that cause distress. It is commonly used to help individuals to overcome phobias or fears of specific situations, such as being in closed spaces, etc.	– Exposure therapy – Aversion therapy
Psychodynamic therapy	Looks at someone's past experiences (events, relationships) to identify how this may inadvertently or unconsciously affect the way the individual feels, thinks and behaves today.	– Freudian psychoanalysis – Psychodynamic family therapy – Brief psychodynamic therapy
Humanistic therapy	Focuses on human potential and self-discovery. It seeks to help an individual to reach their full potential, often by identifying a strong sense of self, exploring strengths, finding meanings.	– Client-centred therapy – Existential therapy

Type of therapy	Description	Examples
Mindfulness-based approaches	Will guide a person to direct their focus on the present moment and cultivate mindfulness, accepting their thoughts and feelings without judgement.	– Mindfulness-based cognitive therapy (MBCT) – Acceptance and commitment therapy (ACT)
Interpersonal therapy	Addresses interpersonal issues and relationships. It will help a person to develop social skills to deal more effectively with others.	– Dynamic interpersonal therapy (DIT)

For the biggest part of the twentieth century, the field of psychotherapy was dominated by single schools. Therapists were trained in one tradition (such as psychoanalysis or behaviourism) and then operated within its theoretical framework.

Guess what? It was also a period of fierce rivalry between the schools. Just like martial artists in the locker rooms, psychotherapists posed similar kinds of questions, which concerned only their field: Which type of therapy is best? What method would work better? Who knows more: Sigmund Freud or B. F. Skinner?

Each one claimed that they had found the best treatment method. The therapists rigidly adhered to the ideas of their schools and vigorously challenged those who decided to adopt a different approach. It was all based around a philosophy of 'my school is better than your school', 'my teacher is smarter than yours', and 'we know more than you'.

Funnily enough, when psychoanalysis was still the single form of psychotherapy, Freud started to clash with his own students. Then, when behaviourism came on the scene, behaviourists began to wrestle with psychoanalysts. Soon afterwards, heated debates took place between behaviourists, humanists and cognitivists. And all of them conflicted with psychoanalysts.

If you look at many of the academic articles written in the 1960s and '70s, you will see a very clear pattern that many of those papers followed. The first paragraph was used to talk about how some school of thought understood and addressed a certain problem. And the rest of the paper was meant to trash it, pointing out how ridiculous it was and how some other type of therapy was better.

I have no doubt that if those therapists had been able to resolve their controversies in a real fight in the 'octagon' (the MMA ring), many would have taken their chance. In that reality, we would probably have seen something like Freud vs Jung, Rogers vs Skinner, maybe Beck vs Ellis in the finals.*

---

* Sigmund Freud is the founder of psychoanalysis. Carl Jung is a psychoanalyst and developer of analytical psychology, a type of psychoanalytic therapy. Burrhus Frederic Skinner is one of the key theorists of the behaviourist school. Carl Rogers is the founder of the humanistic approach and person-centred psychotherapy. Aaron Beck is one of the founders of the cognitive school and developer of cognitive behavioural therapy (CBT). Albert Ellis is a representative of the cognitive school and founder of rational emotive behaviour therapy (REBT).

Yes, it may sound brutal. But on the other hand, the guys could have quickly determined whose kung fu was stronger, couldn't they?

Enter integration. Luckily, things started to change around the early 1980s, without a single drop of blood shed on the mat. At that point, a growing number of therapists began to show a sincere interest in what other approaches could actually offer with regard to treatment (especially when more research papers with empirical findings started to appear). Moreover, some practitioners were increasingly willing to draw ideas or techniques from other approaches to see whether it could make sense for the work they were doing. It was the rise of the so-called 'integrative' movement in psychotherapy.

It all started as informal talks between colleagues. In the early 1980s, Marvin Goldfried (a cognitive-behaviourist) and Paul Wachtel (a psychoanalyst) started to meet once in a while to discuss the similarities and differences between the existing therapies of that time, and to discuss whether it was possible to integrate at least some approaches. As the old legend goes, when Marvin moved to New York, Paul and he started having lunch together. They used to have many exciting discussions, which sometimes extended outside the restaurant to the sidewalks of New York City. At some point, two therapists who represented opposing camps realised that their relationship got too serious for a lunchtime – the lunch was over, but there were still lots of things to talk about. So the guys started meeting for dinner. But even that was not enough. After a year or two of getting kicked out of restaurants at closing time, Marvin and Paul came to believe that more formal and serious steps needed to be taken.

They went through their professional networks and compiled a list of colleagues who were likely to be interested in the rapprochement between the therapies. It turned out that there were a lot of like-minded people, and the list quickly increased to 162 names. After that, everyone agreed that it was time to create a formal organisation that would facilitate the contacts among its members. And in 1983, the Society for the Exploration of Psychotherapy Integration (SEPI) was founded.

The primary goal of SEPI was to create a safe place for an open, collegial dialogue for researchers and practitioners from different backgrounds. At that time, the competition between different schools of therapy was still high, and many societies would react quite negatively to the idea of developing close bonds with other approaches. When interviewed today, Marvin recalls sometimes, for example, how Terry Wilson, who was president of the Association for Advancement of Behavior Therapy in the early 1980s, spent a large part of his presidential address talking about what Marvin was doing and 'how bad the idea was'. It was especially awkward for Marvin, who was present during that speech, sitting there with his colleagues and wondering whether such 'trash talk' was ever required.

Other than that, the mission of SEPI was, of course, to further the exploration of the topic of integration in psychotherapy. Some of the SEPI members were (and remain) professionals who clearly identified themselves with a single school of therapy but admitted that other approaches had something to offer. Others were interested in discovering what ingredients different therapies had in common.* Some wanted to know whether there was a way to integrate existing schools of therapy into a single approach. Still others, who were more research-oriented, set their sights on even bigger things – developing a novel and more comprehensive approach to therapy.

It should be noted that integrative psychotherapy did not exist at that time. And very few people actually understood what integration was all about. But it seems that the direction was clear for everyone: combine and optimise.

There were a number of reasons why the integrative movement quickly caught on among researchers and practitioners. I will mention just two significant factors.

First, there was a growing agreement that no single school of psychotherapy was comprehensive enough to address all the problems, all types of clients, and all the circumstances. Many therapists were increasingly aware that the single-school approaches, in which they had been originally trained, simply had limitations or even were inadequate in certain cases. Therefore, many professionals decided to look beyond and across the theoretical boundaries of their schools to see what could be learned from other 'masters'. The basic motivation was just to increase the efficacy and applicability of their therapeutic skills.

---

* It is about identifying the so-called 'common factors'. Common factors are elements or processes that cut across various therapies and ensure the successful treatment outcome. One example of a common factor is a 'therapeutic alliance'. This refers to the development of working relationships between a counsellor and a client (which is a crucial part of all therapies).

Second, the integration trend was also fuelled by socio-economic factors. In many Western countries – in the United States, for instance – psychotherapy is at least partially covered by insurance companies. Naturally, they seek quick and cost-effective solutions. No insurer would want to pay for years of conversations on the couch or for therapies that had little empirical support. In short, at some point, the business created a clear demand in the market: from now on, the therapy should be short-term, problem-focused and evidence-based. As a result, this created a challenge for many types of psychotherapy, in particular psychodynamic and humanistic approaches.* Basically, many therapists were left with a choice: they could either stay within their single schools and be less in-demand, and, as a result, lag behind their competitors; or they could go and learn from other approaches to improve the quality of their work and shorten its duration, which would help them to stay in the game. Needless to say, many preferred the latter option.

It did not take long, as you might have guessed, for integrative therapy to become an independent school in its own right. Some researchers developed the concepts and explained what integration was. Others suggested the frameworks for how this kind of therapy could be conducted. More and more therapists were eager to be trained in a number of different approaches. And at a certain point, many Western universities simply introduced graduate courses in integrative psychotherapy, along with traditional counselling programmes such as CBT or psychodynamic therapy.

---

* Psychodynamic therapy is notorious for its long-term treatment.

In less than two decades, integrative therapy became one of the most common types of psychotherapy and counselling worldwide. According to surveys, the number of therapists who identify themselves as integrative ranges from around 20 per cent to more than 50 per cent across different countries.

For example, in 1999, Hollanders and McLeod conducted a survey of more than 300 counsellors and therapists in the UK, drawn from various professional associations. The survey found that as many as 87 per cent of the participants took a 'non-pure' approach to therapy. Almost half (49 per cent) of the participants defined themselves as being explicitly integrative (those who intentionally use a mix of intervention strategies), while another 38 per cent reported themselves as being implicitly integrative (i.e. they identify themselves with a single school but also acknowledge the influence of other approaches on their practice).

So, what is integrative therapy anyway? As the name suggests, it is a form of therapy that integrates or combines elements of different therapies. Things that can be combined are techniques, methods or concepts. An integrative therapist (or an integrationist) is basically free to use the most effective techniques available in the field to address their client's needs and problems. For example, one may use cognitive techniques, mindfulness, meditation practices, psychodynamic techniques, and any other tool (as long as it has a scientific basis, of course), as and when appropriate.

To put it simply, integrative therapy is *therapeutic MMA*. Just like a mixed martial artist uses more than one style of fighting, an integrative therapist is a professional who uses more than one style of therapy in his or her practice, when needed.

The central tenet of the integrative approach is that no single form of therapy is best in all situations. Here is the thing. Studies show that many types of psychotherapy do work. However, in practice, one single therapy does not work for every person. If a certain therapy worked perfectly for you, for example, it might not necessarily work for other people. One explanation of this situation is that each person is unique and distinctive. People bring different genetic make-ups, issues and backgrounds when they come to a therapist. For this reason, some techniques of therapy may be effective for some, but may not be as effective for others.

Relatedly, the second big idea behind the integrative approach is that a combination of techniques can work best (rather than being grounded just in one 'pure' approach). Basically, integrationists believe that subscribing just to one approach is too limiting. You can learn some good techniques in one school or another, but you never know whether this one style of therapy will be enough to help you win in the next therapeutic bout. What is the alternative? The alternative is to become a well-rounded specialist. If you have a diverse set of skills, you are able to design a therapy that will suit a wide range of people and contexts.

This philosophy arguably makes integrative therapy the most flexible, adaptable and inclusive approach to treatment (as compared to traditional, singular types of therapy). If a session does not go as planned, for example, a therapist can quickly switch between the techniques and try something else (the flexibility and adaptability aspect). In addition, a therapist can address one, or a wide range, of your needs (the inclusivity aspect). For example, your therapy plan might focus on relationship issues but also address the problem of chronic stress. Want to know how to overcome a phobia? No problem, can be done. Want also to discuss some spiritual or existential questions, such as meaning in life? No worries, there is a tool for that too.

Essentially, what integrative therapists do is that they tailor or customise therapy to each specific person based on their needs or concerns (instead of tailoring a person to the frames of a specific therapy). Here is how it works, in brief. At first, a therapist will carefully assess your characteristics – such as age, personality, cultural background, needs, problems – to determine which combination of techniques might work best for you. Then, using this knowledge, the therapist designs an individual therapy plan that is suited to your personal needs and problems. It is noteworthy that this treatment plan will be individual in each case (as it is tailored specifically to each client's circumstances).

MMA AND INTEGRATIVE THERAPY

What could martial arts and psychotherapy possibly have in common? I may be prejudiced, because I have some background in both fields, but it looks like there are surprisingly many parallels.

In both cases, initially, there were many schools that believed their methods (either of fighting or treatment) to be the very best in the field. Then they started to clash with one another, trying to prove the dominance of their 'style' (some in a ring, while others in academic papers). After that, many practitioners came to understand that no single-school approach had all the answers or was the most effective in all situations. And the outcome? They started to mix and optimise (combining fighting techniques, in one case, and treatment techniques, in the other).

It is also interesting that in just two decades both MMA and integrative therapy have developed from marginalised approaches into popular and mainstream practices. They have also become one of the fastest-growing sports and therapies, as more practitioners keep flocking towards mixed styles over the traditional, pure approaches.

There is no big surprise in the rise of popularity of mixed styles. As I mentioned earlier, when you remain open-minded, willing to learn from any master, and constantly looking for new ways to improve your style, there is literally no limit as to how far you can go.

THE WAY

Just as there are no identical MMA fighters, there are no identical integrative therapists. Even though there is some common ground in general approach and philosophy of direction, which I tried to outline above, there are still differences in training programmes, in understanding of what techniques need to be learned, and so on. To be fair, the divergence of opinion can be found in any sport or professional field.

Let's imagine that you joined my own 'MMA self-care gym'. I belong to the camp of more or less research-oriented integrative practitioners. It means that I am interested not only in applying a wide range of therapeutic techniques, but also in developing new theoretical frameworks that one could use to practise the integrative approach.

Primarily, the goal of such frameworks is to bring some order and clear guidance for integrative self-care or therapy. If a framework is clean and consistent enough, you won't feel lost in this chaos of different approaches and will know what to do, how, when and why.

Additionally, I find it useful when a framework can also shed light on some theoretical questions, such as how our mind functions, what factors shape our personality, what conditions contribute to our mental wellbeing or mental issues, and even on some philosophical questions (e.g. whether people have free will).* My deep belief is that self-understanding or self-knowledge can be therapeutic in itself. I remember when I was still an undergraduate student and we learned something new about how our brain functioned, I was always kind of 'Wow, that's why ...?!' After that, it was always much easier for me to keep calm or pull myself together after stressful situations.

With regard to integration itself, I do not intend to synthesise two or more theories in their pure form. I am more interested in preserving the most valuable insights, concepts or methods of some of the major schools, while always being keen to create something new.

Further in this book, I will put forward one such integrative framework, which I have dubbed the Pyramid

---

* See, for example, *Freedom, Responsibility, and Therapy* (2020), Vlad Beliavsky, Palgrave Macmillan.

Model. It is just one of the many ways the integrative approach may look.

OVERVIEW OF THE MODEL

The Pyramid Model consists of six interconnected parts that are responsible for six key mental functions: reason, beliefs, memories, emotions, speech and behaviour. Each of these six parts of the mind uniquely contributes to who you are and affects your mental wellbeing, physical health, relationships and daily performance.

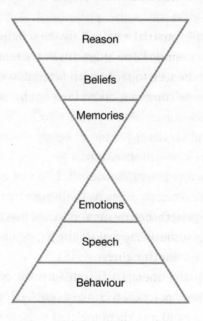

There are proven ways or guidelines for how to manage each of these parts of the mind effectively. Unfortunately, most of us do not know these guidelines, and for this reason we often make 'mental mistakes' when we try to manage ourselves, which often steers us in the wrong direction and causes issues in our performance, health and relationships.

The model suggests that it is important to adjust all six areas of our mind to achieve optimal wellbeing, sense of happiness and performance. In other words, we should take the *integrative* or holistic approach to navigate our inner world.

──────── **Introduction summary** ────────

- What could martial arts and psychotherapy possibly have in common? The short answer is that a similar trend can be seen today in both fields: to combine and optimise. In combat sport, we see a surge in popularity of mixed martial arts (MMA), which is frequently called the world's fastest-growing sport; while in psychotherapy we observe a growing popularity of the so-called integrative approach.

- Integrative therapy is a form of therapy that combines and fuses together elements and techniques from other types of psychotherapy (such as CBT, psychodynamic therapy, humanistic therapy, etc.).

- An integrative therapist is trained to apply the most effective and practical techniques of therapy available in the field and mix them together to form one coherent approach to treatment. It enables the therapist to be flexible enough to deal with a variety of therapeutic situations and design a treatment plan that is best suited for their client's needs.

- Integrative therapy is one of the most common forms of therapy nowadays. According to some surveys, 20 to 50 per cent of therapists report that they use a combination of methods in their practice, rather than sticking just to one 'pure' approach.

- In this book, we will use the Pyramid Model as a framework both to understand our mind a little bit better and to practise integrative self-care.

Part One

The Pyramid Model

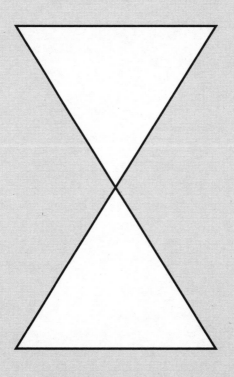

1

The Basics

The Origin of Pyramids

THE PYRAMID MODEL

The brain is the most complex biological structure known to scientists. Some regions or areas of the brain can perform more than one function, including thinking, speech, memory, motor functions and so on. Moreover, some areas can sometimes even change their roles. This may happen, for instance, if there is a head trauma, and the brain tries to compensate for the damage and adapt to new conditions.

Since the human brain is so complicated, it sometimes makes sense to consider simplified models of how our mind is organised. Psychologists, in particular, often come up with metaphors, diagrams or simplified representations that are much more straightforward and accessible for the general public for self-understanding, self-care or therapeutic purposes, than working with MRI brain scans.

In this book, my suggestion is to consider the mind in

the form of the double pyramid. The Pyramid Model consists of six interconnected levels: reason, beliefs, memories, emotions, speech and behaviour.

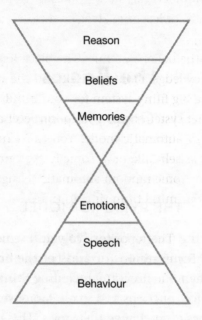

Basically, I artificially divide the way in which the mind functions into six key themes. From a neuroscientific point of view, it is far from accurate (as it is not what our brain looks like). But, for our purposes here, it will give us a good working model.

Let's take a brief overview of each level of the Pyramid Model for more clarity.

1. *Reason* (or the conscious mind) – Reason is responsible for higher mental functions, such as attention,

perception, awareness, critical thinking, planning, decision-making, self-control, etc. Any intentional action involves your conscious mind. It could be dialling a number, calculating, deciding where to go on weekends, or learning a yoga asana.

2. *Beliefs* (the belief system) – The place for your beliefs and knowledge about yourself and the world. Think of it as a big filing system for your mind. In addition, the belief system helps you to interpret and evaluate events in automatic mode. You can experience this process as self-talk, or as some background thinking, or just as some random automatic thoughts that pop up in your mind from time to time.

3. *Memories* – The repository of your memories of past events. For example, it could be recalling what you ate today for breakfast, reminiscing about your graduation day, or how you drove a car for the first time.

4. *Emotions* – The home of your emotions, inborn emotional responses (such as the fight-or-flight response), learned emotional responses (e.g. phobias, emotional associations) and urges. This system makes it possible for a person to have a rich emotional life, experiencing joy, surprise, fear, sadness, anger and so on.

5. *Speech* – The home of your verbal habits. This system helps you to communicate verbally with others – to articulate sounds, tell stories, etc.

6. *Behaviour* – The repository of all your motor habits. A habit is an action that we do repeatedly and automatically, without a thought. How early you get up, what you have for breakfast, how you dress, how you walk, how you sit, and how often you check your phone, are all examples of habits.

TWO PYRAMIDS

You may wonder: why a double pyramid as the framework? Here are three main reasons:

1. *Inward view: conscious vs unconscious* – When you consider your own mind – when you introspect and look inward to examine your own thoughts, emotions, memories, etc. – you may discover that some information is more conscious and more easily accessible to you, while other information is much more unconscious and hidden. The short answer is that the top pyramid of the model consists of levels of the mind that are more conscious, whereas the bottom pyramid consists of levels that are largely unconscious (Chapter 2 will explain the subject in more detail).

2. *Outward view: visible vs concealed* – When you want to understand another person better – and take a look at how they behave, how they express themselves, etc. – you may realise that again not all information is equally available to you. But in this case, the situation will be reversed. When we observe other

people, the levels of the bottom pyramid are much more observable, apparent and clearly expressed for us, whereas the levels of the top pyramid are largely concealed.

For example, we can clearly see how other people behave. We can also hear them speaking. And we can notice when other individuals experience strong emotions, feel happy, or sad, or scary, or angry, for example, even if they try to force back their feelings or to hide them for whatever reason.

By contrast, the levels of the top pyramid look much more veiled from external observation. We can't see, for example, what other people remember or what they went through in their life. We can't see what they know or what they believe in. We may notice that a person is thinking about something, even make an educated guess what about, and even be right sometimes, but we can't be always 100 per cent sure what they are actually thinking about.

3. *Different dimensions of mental health* – Integrative therapists are trained to deal with multiple dimensions or aspects of mental health (see Introduction for more details on the integrative approach). Typically, integrative therapists take into account the cognition, emotions and behaviour of their clients. In other words, a therapist considers how clients think, what they feel and how they behave. The thing is that cognition, emotions and behaviour are just about the most important factors that affect our mental health.

In short, when we consider the Pyramid Model, we can identify those different dimensions of mental health. The top pyramid, for example, features the so-called cognitive dimension of mental health. That's because the top pyramid consists of the levels of the mind that have a largely cognitive nature, such as our thinking, storage of our beliefs and memories. By contrast, the bottom pyramid features two other important aspects of mental health and two deeper levels of the mind. These are emotional and behavioural levels (the behavioural level consists of both verbal and motor habits).

SYMBOLISM

There are also two complementary reasons why I use the double pyramid as the framework. These two points may be especially of interest for those who like symbolism as much as I do.

■ *The unity of opposites* – Two pyramids can be viewed as the symbol that represents the idea of harmonious unity of opposites. A close analogy is the yin-yang symbol. Briefly put, the concept of yin-yang is that two opposite or contrary forces are actually interconnected and complementary. Yin is often characterised as a feminine, dark, receptive force, while yang is seen as masculine, bright and active. Though these are two competing opposites, they are also inseparable. Two halves attract one another because of their differences. As they start to interact, it turns out that they can complement each other. In this process, they complete wholeness and create a dynamic system, which is greater than the assembled parts. Ultimately, the interaction of these two forces creates harmony, which gives birth to things.

Now back to the Pyramid Model. From a symbolic point of view, two pyramids that point upward and downward are often thought to represent opposing forces. They are often thought to signify, for example, the earth vs the sky, or male vs female. The whole structure, however, is believed to denote the idea of harmonious unity of opposites (see the Louvre inverted pyramid as an example).*

In our particular case, we can also distinguish two opposing structures: reason (the top level of the top pyramid) and emotion (the top level of the bottom pyramid). When it comes to the mind and neuroscience, it is very common for researchers to distinguish these two brain antagonists: the reason (namely the prefrontal cortex) and emotion (the limbic system,

---

* The Louvre inverted pyramid is a skylight located in the Louvre museum in Paris. It is a massive upside-down glass pyramid. There is also a small stone pyramid that is stationed just below, on the floor, and almost touches the tip of the glass pyramid. The Louvre inverted pyramid featured in Dan Brown's international bestseller *The Da Vinci Code*. The protagonist of the book interpreted the inverted pyramid as a chalice, a feminine symbol, while the stone pyramid was understood as a blade, a masculine symbol. The whole structure was believed to express the idea of the union of the sexes.

including the amygdala). The two structures often compete to gain control over human behaviour: while reason is the origin of self-control and logic, emotion is what issues quick and impulsive responses (e.g. the fight-or-flight response). Nonetheless, the two structures are also highly interdependent. Both are needed for our normal everyday functioning and survival. Life would be a mess if we were devoid either of logical thinking or feeling.

On the whole, I like to think that once a person learns to work with both structures, with both pyramids, this leads to inner harmony, which in turn can give rise to many beautiful things.

First and foremost, I mean the overall sense of mental wellbeing. If you take care of each part of your inner world, and nothing is left behind, you naturally reap the benefits.

But in addition, there may be other valuable results. You may feel the desire to create or build something new, something beautiful or useful. It may be the will to establish and maintain good relationships with others. It may feel like the overall drive to support and develop life around you rather than suppress or destroy it. In short, what I mean is that after reaching harmony within, you will be also naturally inclined to build and maintain harmony outside, in your external, material world.

- *Infinite microcosm* – If you take a look at the whole figure, without dividing it into separate parts, you may recognise that the double pyramid resembles the number 8, which generally stands for the infinity symbol. The scientist in me understands that the brain can be scanned and all processes that happen inside can be revealed and described. But part of me likes to think that the human mind can be viewed as a separate unique world, a microcosm, that can be limitless, abundant and continuously expanding or growing as our external physical universe.

In the following chapters, we will continue exploring the Pyramid Model, in particular, elaborating on the relationships between the different levels. Hopefully, it will help you to understand a little bit better how your mind is organised and how to navigate through your inner world. After that, we will move on to more practical questions to understand how to work with each level of the Pyramid Model to boost your mental health, performance and sense of happiness.

——————— **Chapter summary** ———————

- We will use the so-called Pyramid Model as a framework or working model to understand better how our mind is organised and how to train in integrative self-care.
- The Pyramid Model consists of six levels or areas that cover key mental functions and aspects of mental health: reason, beliefs, memories, emotions, speech and behaviour.

- Each of these six parts of the mind uniquely contributes to who you are and affects your mental wellbeing, physical health, relationships and daily performance.

2

Some Theory

How We Remember Things

MEMORY

A huge part of our mind and personality are related to memory. Think about it – what would your life look like if you did not remember anything? You'd not know who you are, what you like or dislike, what you did yesterday or planned to do tomorrow. You'd not be able to recall how to get dressed, how to walk, or even how to read these words. Actually, you'd not know why you decided to read this book in the first place.

Many people think that our memory is monolithic. It is as if the memory could be compared to a big box or a closet, where you put things and later take them out. However, that's not how it works. In fact, there are many boxes or many areas in the brain that store our memories. What's more, there are also many distinct types of memory – which is one of the most important discoveries in neuroscience.

For example, one region of the brain is used to store your knowledge – that is to say, your memories of facts and beliefs about the world. The other place is used to store your habits – that is, your memories of how to execute different routine behaviours. Yet another place is used to store your memories of past events.

If we take a look at the Pyramid Model, each level of the model, in fact, accommodates a specific type of memory. Before we move forward, I should point out here that the Pyramid Model is not just about memory. One level of the model can entail multiple cognitive functions and processes, as well as memory. The reason system, for example, is responsible for analytical thinking, self-control, attention and consciousness, among other things.

It is important to note here that all these types of memory have a different nature. They have a different mechanism of formation and they serve a different purpose. This implies that we will need different tools or techniques if we want to manage each of those types of memory.

In this chapter, we will get to know about the nature of those different types of memory. And later on, we will learn what methods we can use to make changes in our behaviour and boost our wellbeing. As the American poet John Lancaster Spalding once said: 'As memory may be a paradise from which we cannot be driven, it may also be a hell from which we cannot escape.' Without further ado, let's take a stroll down memory lane.

SHORT-TERM MEMORY VS

LONG-TERM MEMORY

For a start, it makes sense to distinguish between short-term and long-term memory. Short-term memory refers to the capacity to retain a small amount of information in the mind and keep it available for a brief period of time. By contrast, long-term memory stores a wide range of information for a long period of time.

Below, you will find more detailed descriptions. But for now, it will be helpful to see where short-term and long-term memory are located within the Pyramid Model.

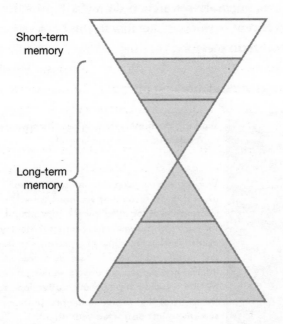

WORKING MEMORY

Working memory refers to the ability to hold and work with information for a short period of time. It is something that holds information in place so that you can work with it briefly and not lose track of what you're doing.

Sometimes the terms working memory and short-term memory are used interchangeably. Though the two concepts overlap significantly, they are not quite the same thing. Short-term memory refers only to the temporary, short-term storage of information. By contrast, working memory refers to the ability not only to store but also to work, use or manipulate information for a short period of time. As many other contemporary researchers do, we will primarily refer to the concept of working memory in this book rather than just short-term memory.

Characteristics of working memory

Explicit (also known as conscious)	Working memory retains information we are currently aware of or thinking of.
Short-term	Working memory can hold information for around 15-30 seconds. If you don't actively retain information in the mind, silently repeating it, for example, you will quickly forget it. Have you ever forgotten the name of a person who was just introduced to you? It is simply because this information slipped out of your working memory. Maybe you did not pay enough attention to the name of that person in the first place, or something just distracted your attention.

Limited capacity	Working memory can keep only a limited amount of information. Though researchers dispute the exact number or amount of 'bytes' that can be held, it is commonly believed that working memory can retain about 5-9 pieces of information at a time. These could be digits, words, thoughts or other units. For example, for most people it would be very hard to multiply 523 by 798. That's because the amount of information that has to be maintained in the mind at once during this calculation exceeds the capacity of working memory of most people.
Active	Not only can working memory store information, but it also allows you to 'work' with this information, manipulating and transforming it. For example, when you have a conversation, you can both remember what was just said and analyse it at the same time, connecting with what you already know.

Examples of working memory

- Remembering the name of a person who has been just introduced to you
- Remembering a phone number (or a password, address, appointment date) that was just told to you while looking for a pen to write it down
- Remembering what you want to say until another person finishes talking
- Remembering a question asked by someone while thinking about it and formulating an answer
- Keeping in mind the list of grocery items you need to put in your basket at the supermarket
- Remembering the correct amount of ingredients

that you need to add (e.g. three potatoes, 200g of cheese, two tablespoons of flour) after reading the recipe a few minutes ago

- Remembering what the text is all about when you have just read a few paragraphs but are no longer looking at the page
- Remembering and following the directions that contain multiple steps (e.g. 'Go along the road. Turn left at the crossroads. Go past the cinema.')
- Keeping in mind numbers while calculating how much the bill will be for the dishes you've ordered at a restaurant.

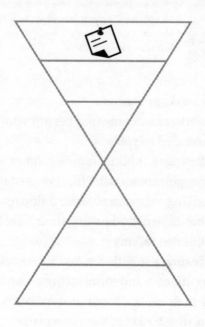

Think of working memory as a sort of sketchpad or temporary sticky note in your head. If you don't have any external place to record information, such as a phone or a piece of paper, then you will rely on your working memory.

You may also notice that working memory is used for the things that are important to you right now, not tomorrow. It usually holds information that is required to complete a certain task here and now. You are doing something or working on a task, and your mind keeps relevant information readily available for you during this time.

Working memory plays one of the central roles in our mental life. It helps us to learn and complete any basic task, such as reading, reasoning, planning, understanding complex issues, following a conversation, guiding your behaviour, choosing between a few options, doing mental arithmetic, etc.

Consider reading as an example. As you are reading this sentence, you can keep in mind what you just read and also place it into the wider context of the rest of the chapter.

Another good example is mental arithmetic. Suppose you need to add 14 and 15 in your head, without being able to use a pen and paper or a calculator. To start with, you would need to hold these two numbers in your working memory. Then you would need to retrieve from long-term memory the knowledge needed to solve maths problems (basic arithmetic rules – how to add numbers, in particular), bringing this new chunk of information to your working memory. After that, you would add together the numbers and find the correct answer: 29. This will be another bit of information that you need to keep in mind temporarily.

To sum up, working memory is what allows you to visualise or to 'see' 14 and 15 in your head at first. Then it enables you to remember the correct answer, 29, for some time so that you can write it down or use it for some other operation.

You may forget any of these numbers in five minutes, or even in thirty seconds. And that's totally fine. You have already finished the task. Your working memory has successfully fulfilled its short-term role so you can move on to something else.

Note again that working memory is a temporary or short-term store. It is being updated continuously – with new information coming in, decaying and being quickly replaced by other data. If information fades from working memory, it is gone for ever and it cannot be retrieved. In fact, this is what happens with most of the content of working memory daily – it is just being moved to your 'mental rubbish bin'.

That said, there is also an option to retain information for longer periods. Working memory is sort of a gateway into the so-called long-term memory. If you make a conscious effort to memorise something, you can transfer information from working memory into your long-term storage. Repeat it enough, for example, and the memory will become more permanent.

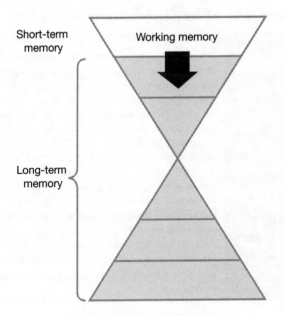

LONG-TERM MEMORY

Long-term memory refers to the storage of information for a long period. Most information that we encounter every day dissipates unless it is transferred into long-term memory, our memory bank.

Basically, long-term memory refers to anything you remember that happened more than a few minutes ago. These are those memories that you can recall days, months, years and even decades after they were originally stored.

Characteristics of long-term memory

Durable/ long-term	What distinguishes long-term memories is that they are relatively enduring, even though they are also susceptible to being forgotten. Long-term memories can last for days, years or even for a whole life. You may recall, for example, what you ate yesterday for breakfast as well as how it felt when you fell off a bike in your childhood.
Below awareness	Unlike working memory, long-term memories lie outside your conscious mind. You are not typically aware of what is in your long-term memory until you need to recall some information. But when needed, these memories (at least some of them) can be called or drawn into your conscious mind (into your working memory).

Right now, you may not be thinking, for example, of what you had yesterday for lunch or what time you woke up today. But if asked, you'd be able to access these memories and bring them into your conscious awareness. Equally, you don't walk around constantly thinking of grammar rules, your plans for the next week, or how to use your online banking app. But you can retrieve this information upon request.

Metaphorically, you can access a certain saved folder and retrieve what you're looking for – be it the year of your birth, the name of the current president of the United States, or what time you're supposed to meet your friends in the evening.

It should be noted, however, that not all long-term

memories are created equal. Some memories are relatively easy to recall, while others require prompts or reminders to be accessed. Some memories spring to mind quite regularly, while others can remain silent for years.

There are many different forms of long-term memory. Some can contain beliefs and knowledge, episodes from your personal life, as well as more implicit types of information such as the memory of how to complete a certain task or what things to be cautious of.

It is generally accepted among psychologists that long-term memory can be divided into four main types:

Long-term memory	– Semantic memory (knowledge) – Episodic memory (past events) – Emotional memory (emotional associations) – Procedural memory (habits)

Each of these types of memory has its own place in the Pyramid Model, as it can be shown overleaf. In the following sections, we will get familiar with each type of long-term memory individually and explore them in more detail.

NB: I subdivide procedural memory into two types: procedural motor memory (motor habits) and procedural verbal memory (verbal habits). It is the only difference, when compared with the traditional approach.

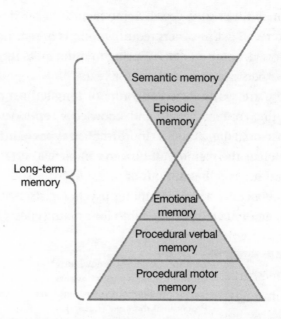

EPISODIC MEMORY

Episodic memory is your memory of specific events, episodes or situations from your personal past. Recalling the first time you drove a car is an example.

Actually, episodic memory is what most people think of when they use or hear the term 'memory'. That's why, for the sake of simplicity, when referring to this level of the mind, I may also use the general term 'memory'.

Episodic memories consist of your own vision (as these events happened to you and not someone else), contextual information (time, place), the experience, and often an emotion associated with this event (how it made you feel). When you recall any episodic memories, it feels as if you've mentally travelled back in time and revisited your past history.

Imagine that you bump into some random guy in the street. You cast a glance at him, apologise and keep walking. But having made a few steps, you stop. Something feels very familiar. You turn around and suddenly realise that it is your old schoolmate Bob. And before you know it, you shout, 'Hey mate!' You then get together for a cup of coffee and spend several hours reminiscing about the good old days at school.

Examples of episodic memory
- recalling what you did this morning
- remembering your first kiss
- reminiscing about your first day at work
- recalling how you spent your last holiday
- remembering the face of your ex
- remembering where you put your keys
- who came for your birthday last year
- what you felt when your favourite team won the championship
- the last time you felt happy
- how it feels to pet your friend's dog
- how you came across this book
- while sleeping, you recall an episode from your school years, of getting called on in a class when you were unprepared
- while sitting at an Asian restaurant and looking over the menu, you suddenly recall how you tried a very tasty tom yum soup some time ago at another place

- having a flashback (e.g. a military scene in a movie causes a combat veteran to involuntarily begin to recall his friends die on the battlefield).

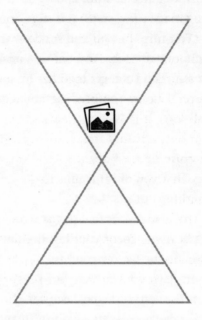

One important thing to keep in mind is that episodic memories often involve emotional experiences. When we recall an event, we can record not only the details of the event itself (the time, the context, what happened) but also the emotions that we experienced during this event.

For this reason, remembering a situation or a person from the past is often accompanied by various feelings. Recalling your ex, for example, may evoke the feeling of love, resentment, sadness, gratitude, or all those things at once. Or recalling the episodes from your childhood – let's say how you goofed around with your best friends or rode a bike for the first time – may evoke a shiver of excitement or nostalgia. Even years later, we can still feel those emotions as intensely as we did the first time.

Why do emotions merge with our memories? One explanation is that emotions help us to remember things better. If an event is 'colourless', containing information that is pretty mundane or neutral, we don't tend to pay much attention to it. So it is pretty easy to forget such events. But when it comes to emotions, it is a whole new ball game. We are far more likely to notice things that arouse emotions – be they positive or negative. Emotions attach significance to events. As a result, we are wired to remember things that bring good or painful emotions.

Most of the time, this mechanism serves us well. However, it all depends on the dose or extent of those emotions. Sometimes we may face a highly emotionally-charged event – a near-death experience or trauma such as an assault, domestic violence, childhood abuse, military combat, a car accident, escaping from a deadly fire and so on. In any such case, we experience extremely strong negative emotions, which fix these terrible events in our memory.

At best, you may just form a disturbing memory of that event. It may bubble up occasionally, reminding you of how bad you felt at that time (e.g. scared, disappointed, ashamed, etc.). We all have something in our past that brought us some pain or discomfort – hurtful words said by a school bully, an embarrassing moment at work, losing a loved one. All of those things could have happened years ago, and you do not want to think about them. Yet they may still come back to haunt you from time to time.

At worst, when people go through a scary, shocking or dangerous event, they may develop symptoms of PTSD (post-traumatic stress disorder). In PTSD, a person suffers from recurrent reminders of a traumatic event – such as intrusive thoughts, nightmares, flashbacks – and struggles to readjust to normal life.

Flashbacks can be particularly distressing. These are involuntary, recurring and powerful kinds of memories. In a flashback, you basically relive a past event or fragment of past experience. You may maintain some connection with the reality or just lose any awareness of what is going on around you, being transported back to your traumatic event. As a result, you may feel as if the traumatic event is happening again, which often leads to panic, numbness or defensive behaviours. Unfortunately, people often fail to recognise that they are having a flashback. For example, a war veteran might begin to feel that they are back on the battlefield, re-experiencing explosions, gunfire or the death of fellow soldiers. And this can all be triggered by such seemingly trivial and innocent things as watching a war scene on TV or hearing a car backfire.

SEMANTIC MEMORY

Semantic memory refers to the memory of ideas, facts and concepts. It includes all the things that can be referred to as general knowledge, which you have accumulated throughout your life.

More specifically, semantic memory stores general facts (e.g. that a year consists of twelve months), concepts (mathematical formulas, cooking recipes), rules (understanding of how to behave in a restaurant, when it is safe to cross a street), values (to be brave, to be caring), vocabulary (what the French word 'bonjour' means in English), beliefs about yourself (understanding your strengths and weaknesses), and beliefs about the world.

Consider an example. Someone asks: 'When did people first land on the Moon?' You say: 'In 1969.' How do you know the answer? The answer comes from your semantic memory. You may have learned this fact in school or read about it somewhere. Your semantic memory had retained this information and then provided this information to you upon request.

Examples of semantic memory

- knowing the name of the first president of the United States
- knowing the colour of zebras
- knowing what a pen is used for
- the number of days in a year
- who sang 'Bohemian Rhapsody'
- where Australia is located on the map
- what Roman numerals VI and XII mean
- knowing the answer to 2 × 2
- knowing how to make the past tense in a sentence
- vocabulary (e.g. understanding what the English words 'New Year', 'table' and 'truck' mean)
- remembering historic dates (e.g. when the Second World War ended)

- what your home address is
- the date you were born
- what your mother's name is
- remembering the tasks on your to-do list
- recollecting the time for a doctor's appointment.

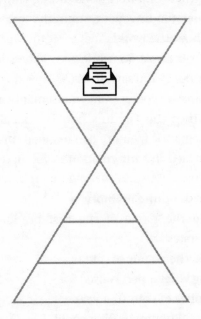

Note that semantic memories are often derived from epi-sodic memories. In other words, we can get knowledge from our past personal experiences. This is especially common in childhood when we deal with new things for the very first time. Learning how to use a remote control, for example, can start with the experience of pushing a button by chance. This experience can then be transformed into knowledge and stored in your semantic memory.

However, it is also possible to have semantic memory without episodic memory. For example, you can forget the time when you played with the remote control for the first time, but you can retain the acquired knowledge of how to use it. You may also know, for instance, that you went to the first grade when you were six or seven (have semantic memory), but you may have forgotten the event itself: what the weather was like, how you met your first teacher, what your first class was about, or how you felt that day (no episodic memory).

PROCEDURAL MEMORY - MOTOR

Procedural memory is the memory of how to do things. It refers to all skills, habits and behaviours (procedures) you have ever learned.

Examples of procedural memory
- knowing how to walk
- how to do push-ups
- how to navigate a familiar area (such as your apartment or neighbourhood)
- how to swim
- how to brush your teeth
- how to play a musical instrument (e.g. guitar, piano, drums)
- how to tie shoe laces
- how to play a familiar video game
- how to write
- how to chop an onion

- how to type on a keyboard
- scrolling on your phone
- tapping your foot to the beat of a song
- hitting a ball with a tennis racket
- checking the wing mirrors for other vehicles before changing lanes.

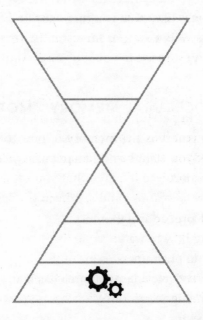

When you do some action for the very first time, you use your conscious mind. You pay attention, exert self-control, and spend much mental resource overall. But if you perform this action repeatedly and over a prolonged period of time, it can then turn into a habit. It becomes so ingrained in your mind that you don't need to think of how to do it any more. You just do it.

You don't have to consciously recall how to carry out any of these tasks. If you want to walk, you just walk and don't think of how to move your legs. When you get into your car, you don't remind yourself how to start the car, how to use the indicators or how to pull over. The procedural memory takes over and you can perform these tasks with little or no thought.

I guess you've heard many times before that habits are important for wellbeing and success in life. It should probably come as no surprise to you, but I still want to make this point clear.

The fact that habits are repetitive is what makes them so powerful and impactful. Simply put, what you do every day, from year to year, has a constant and increasing impact on you. Suppose you ate a bag of crisps today. There is no big harm in that. But let's imagine that you eat a bag of crisps every day for a year. Would it affect your weight? Your health? That is a rhetorical question.

In this context, it is common to distinguish between two main types of habits – bad habits and good habits. While good habits help us achieve our goals and a high quality of life, bad habits block our progress and often harm our wellbeing.

The last thing I should mention is that knowledge (semantic memory) may exist independently from our habits (procedural memory). For example, when, as a kid, you first notice a bike in the street, you may learn what the bike is, how it works, how to put on the brakes, how to adjust a seat, and how to turn. You then may keep this knowledge for the rest of your life and never actually try to ride a bike. Or, this initial knowledge can then be followed by practice. You pluck up courage, sit on a bike, and pedal, trying to keep your balance and not to fall.

PROCEDURAL (VERBAL) MEMORY

Procedural memory also plays a significant role in our speech. Let's call it the procedural *verbal* memory to distinguish it from other common procedural memories (motor habits).

Strictly speaking, our language and speech production depends on many systems and regions of the brain. It is definitely not only about memory. But since many aspects of language are learned, it is natural that language also depends heavily on our memory.

Semantic memory, for example, stores our lexical knowledge. This includes our vocabulary, the meaning of words and knowledge of grammar (e.g. understanding how to form past or future tenses, etc.).

The procedural memory, on the other hand, is widely believed to underlie the rules and sequences in language, such as grammar sequences and pronunciation patterns. This way, the procedural memory allows you to speak without giving conscious thought to grammar rules and articulation patterns, such as how to put words in the right order to make a sentence, what tense to use, or how to pronounce words correctly.

Examples of verbal habits

- building a grammatically correct sentence (without consciously thinking of how to do that)
- carrying on a conversation with a friend on autopilot, while thinking about something else
- reciting the alphabet
- singing a familiar song or rhyme
- overusing filler words and phrases – e.g. like, um, ah, you know, actually, basically (people are often completely unaware of this until you point it out)
- speaking a foreign language with an accent (pronouncing foreign sounds and words as you'd habitually do in your native language)
- noticing when someone mispronounces a word.

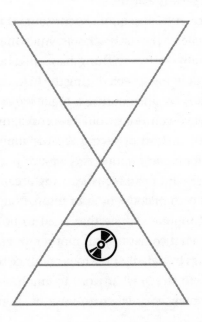

Note the way you speak. Normally, you don't give a conscious thought about how to move your tongue, how to pronounce words correctly, how to change your vocal tone, or how to build a sentence. It all happens on autopilot.

When someone asks you: 'Hey! How are you doing?' you may instinctively reply: 'Good, thanks! You?' even if it is not true, and you are actually having a terrible day. You say so just out of (verbal) habit.

If you have ever learned a foreign language, you know that it is a pretty difficult task. It is important to pay attention to lots of things: how to pronounce unfamiliar sounds, how to use grammar, how to create the right intonation, etc. It is because all languages are different. But when learned, you no longer have to think about all this stuff. It becomes a habit, your second nature.

I remember in high school I spent some time in France, studying in one of the local schools. And when I was back home in Ukraine, a funny thing happened. French words just slipped out in my speech during the first couple of weeks back. For example, once during a literature class a teacher asked me: 'Have you done your home assignments?' And I replied 'Oui', instead of saying 'Yes'. It simply became a verbal habit for me to respond this way.

Another relevant example is learning accents. Each language has its own melody: rules of intonation, articulation patterns and unique sounds that need to be pronounced correctly. When it comes to your mother tongue, you know all these things by default: how to pronounce those sounds, what syllable to stress, what word to emphasise to make a point in a sentence, or when to raise or drop intonation.

You do this automatically when you speak. It is simply part of your memory.

But this body of knowledge can also cause difficulties when you decide to learn a second language. You have probably heard someone who speaks a language with a strong accent. If you ask a foreigner to read a simple English sentence such as 'I have a car', the word 'have' may sound as 'av' if said by a French speaker (because the 'h' sound is always silent in French), or 'haf' if said by a German speaker (because German does not have the 'v' sound at the end of words). On the other hand, English speakers learning German are likely to struggle with a phrase like 'danke schön' (because the 'ö' sound, called the umlaut in German, does not exist in English). Many people will have the urge just to ignore those weird extra dots above the 'o' and pronounce normal English short 'o', saying 'schon' instead of 'schön'.

Why does it happen? One of the reasons is that second-language speakers draw on the verbal habits and unconscious rules that they already know from their native language. We tend to transfer the intonation, pronunciation patterns and grammar rules from our first language into a second one. Basically, procedural memory suggests a habitual way of speech, and we follow it.

EMOTIONAL MEMORY

How do you feel when you hear the pop of a champagne cork? What about when you hear your car alarm going off outside? The first might make you feel excited or even happy. The second might make you scared or annoyed and might make you come out of the house to check whether everything is okay. Why do you think these two sounds can cause two different emotions and even behaviour?

The thing is that people can also acquire emotional memories. Emotional memories are learned (or conditioned) emotional reactions (like fear or excitement), which occur in response to a specific trigger (like hearing the pop of a champagne cork or a car alarm).

Emotional memories are formed by the mechanism that is known as associative learning (also known as classical conditioning). That is when you learn the association between two stimuli – between the so-called neutral stimulus (neutral things that do not trigger any emotion or behaviour on their own) and the unconditioned stimulus (things that trigger a natural, automatic reaction, for example: dust in your nose that causes you to sneeze; or an unexpected loud bang that makes you flinch).

Consider the fear of dogs as an example. Originally a dog is not scary at all (neutral stimulus). But suppose seeing a dog (neutral stimulus) is paired with some painful experience, like being attacked by the dog (unconditioned stimulus). Your brain may then create a strong association between the two things: dogs = pain. If this happens, seeing a dog can elicit fear on its own (conditioned stimulus). So the next time you walk down the road and see a dog – even a friendly one – you may experience fear and the sense of danger.

In any such case, you start to feel fear whenever you encounter anything that reminds you of trauma, even if you consciously understand that the fear is irrational. For example, you may understand rationally that a small dog wagging its tail is not dangerous at all and won't bite you, but still be frightened to be nearby, let alone to pet the dog. Similarly, you may know that a lift in your office is safe and is unlikely to plunge down many floors, but still feel terrified to use it.

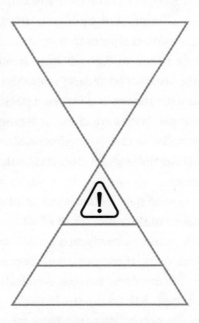

But it is not only about negative emotions. By the same token, we can learn positive emotional associations between two things. It could be, for example, that weekends = joy, pizza = pleasure, etc.

For example, I have a strong positive association that dog = joy. My aunt used to have a beautiful German shepherd, with whom I spent many happy days in my childhood. I still clearly remember, for example, waking up in the morning and seeing his funny furry face staring at me every time. Since then I have been a huge fan of big fluffy dog breeds. Whenever I walk down the street and notice a big pet, I can't help but smile and watch them pass by.

It is interesting that I also had many unpleasant experiences related to dogs. A neighbour's dog bit me once. Another time, I had to run away from a Caucasian shepherd dog, which looked like a wild grizzly bear. A few years later, I had a motorbike accident because of stray dogs. I was riding a motorbike down a narrow road when a pack of stray dogs ran out into my path and gave chase. It was so unexpected that I lost control of the steering wheel and crashed into a pavement. Luckily, nobody got hurt, and the dogs quickly lost interest in me.

Potentially, I could have obtained a fear of dogs or at the very least a dislike of dogs as a result of all those incidents. But, probably because I already had a very strong positive attitude towards dogs, those negative experiences did not have such a significant impact on me. And today I still adore the giant fuzzy pups – the more the better.

It is also worth noting that traumatic memories can be stored in a few memory boxes at the same time. For instance, many people have a fear of rats (emotional memory), screaming and jumping on to chairs whenever they see them. And they may also remember how they happened to acquire this fear (episodic memory). A person may recall, for example, that she was startled by a big rat when she was playing in the backyard in her childhood.

Yet, emotional memories can also exist independently. For instance, a person may have a phobia (emotional memory) but doesn't have a conscious recollection of what formed it (no episodic memory). It is especially common if the traumatic incident happened in early childhood. Back to our previous example. With the passing of many years, the person may simply forget that she saw a big scary rat in her backyard as a child. In other words, her recollections of the incident (episodic memory) could fade and vanish with time. But the acquired fear of rats (emotional memory) formed during this incident may not go anywhere. So, as a result, her fear of rats may persist.

EXPLICIT MEMORY VS IMPLICIT MEMORY

We have covered all key types of memory above. I hope I've managed to explain this quite complex subject clearly, and you are still following. Please stay with me. We've almost done with this theme. There is one last important distinction left that is important to mention.

It is also common to divide long-term memory into two main groups – explicit memory and implicit memory. Explicit memory (also known as declarative memory, knowing 'what') consists of episodic memory and semantic memory. Meanwhile, implicit memory (also known as non-declarative memory, knowing 'how') consists of procedural and emotional memory.

Long-term memory	Explicit memory (also known as declarative memory, knowing 'what')	– semantic memory – episodic memory
	Implicit memory (also known as non-declarative memory, knowing 'how')	– emotional memory – procedural memory (motor, verbal)

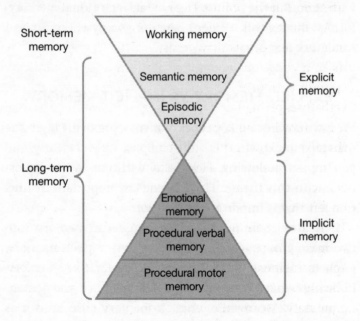

Explicit memory is the memory that can be recalled consciously and intentionally. Imagine, for example, that someone asks you: 'What is the capital of Peru?' Maybe it will come to you immediately if you know geography well or visited Peru lately. But chances are that you need to pause and think about it at least for a second. If you actually know this geography fact, after checking your memory database, you will bring the answer to your conscious awareness.

Explicit memory is also known sometimes as declarative memory, as you can 'declare' or verbalise information that you recall. For instance, you can say: 'The capital of Peru is Lima.' Or you can recall and describe in words how you have spent your latest holidays, maybe in Peru.

As mentioned, explicit memory consists of episodic memory and semantic memory. Partly, that's because you make a conscious attempt to retrieve both semantic and episodic memories. And partly, that's because you can also verbally explain or describe those memories – such as recalling your school graduation ceremony or naming animals that live in Africa.

Implicit memory, by contrast, is the type of memory that is unconscious and unintentional. It means that you don't have to use conscious thought to recall these memories. These are the things that you recall and do automatically, without any strategic effort or intention to use memory. You can remember fairly easily, for example, how to ride a bike, how to walk, or how to put words together to make a grammatically correct sentence.

Implicit memory is also referred to sometimes as non-declarative memory. That's because it is often hard to verbalise or to explain how you do the things you do (habitual tasks), even though you can do them quite easily. You may be very good at riding a bike, for example. But if someone asks you to give step-by-step instructions, you are likely to find it difficult to put it into words. This also applies to the way we speak. If English is your native language, you know, for example, how to do the long /ɜ:/ sound (in words like 'bird', 'work' and 'fur'). But if a foreigner asks you how you actually pronounce this sound, unless you're an English teacher, it might be hard for you to explain. You just do it, and you never think of the position that your jaw, lips or tongue are in at this moment.

Implicit memory includes procedural memory and emotional memory. On the one hand, you don't need to try to recall consciously how to do routine stuff or how to be cautious or excited about certain things. These memories come to you automatically. When you make a bed, for example, you don't need to conjure up each step that needs to be completed. When you sing a favourite song, you don't think ahead about the words to the song or an appropriate vocal tone. Or if you are afraid of dogs, you don't need to specifically recall how to avoid dogs. All of these memories will come to you naturally. On the other hand, it is also quite hard to verbalise both procedural and emotional memories. If I ask a person with a phobia why they have fear of heights, for example, many of them may find it difficult to explain or describe this mechanism.

Do you remember when I was explaining my choice of the double pyramid as a framework (see Chapter 1)? I've mentioned that the top pyramid consists of levels of the mind that are generally conscious, whereas the bottom pyramid accommodates levels that are largely unconscious. Now I can be more specific. In essence, the top pyramid is the home of different explicit (or conscious) types of memory, whereas the bottom pyramid is where we locate different implicit (or unconscious) types of memory.

Before we wrap up this section, there is one last thing. It is worth noting that researchers distinguish between explicit and implicit memory normally just in the context of long-term memory. But you can read elsewhere that essentially working memory is also an explicit type of memory. That's because we are, in fact, fully aware of the content of working memory and can easily declare information that it holds. It might even be said that working memory is the most explicit one.

There is no divergence of opinion here. It is fine to talk about explicit memory just in the context of long-term memory. And it is also useful to keep in mind that working memory is also conscious in nature. Either way, it is fair to say that the top pyramid is the home of different forms of explicit memory, whereas the bottom pyramid is all about implicit memory.

─────────── **Chapter summary** ───────────

- Memories are not formed and stored in a single part of the brain. Instead, there are many different types of memory, which are stored in different regions of the brain.
- Working memory is a system with limited capacity that allows us to hold information temporarily and work with it.

- Long-term memory is the system that stores information for a long period of time.
- Long-term memory comprises four main types – episodic memory (past events), semantic memory (facts, knowledge), procedural memory (habits and skills) and emotional memory (emotional associations).

About Traumas

When Some Part of the Mind Fails

THE DISCOVERY OF DIFFERENT TYPES OF MEMORY

How do we know about all those different types of memory? The discovery of explicit and implicit memory originates from the treatment of patients who suffered from amnesia. After years of observation, researchers detected that while a person may lose some type of memory due to a trauma or disease, they can still retain some memory abilities.

AMNESIA

Have you ever forgotten where you left your phone? Or have you struggled to remember the name of an actor, even though you watched lots of their movies? Or consider this situation: you walk into a kitchen and forget what you were supposed to do there. You stop and think to yourself: 'Why did I come in here?' Well, you are not alone. All healthy people forget things once in a while. Forgetting is a normal part of how the brain works. But some people have a hard time remembering things almost all the time.

Amnesia is a partial or total memory loss caused by brain trauma or disease. Though amnesia is often described in movies as a total loss of one's identity, in reality such cases are very rare. There are two common types of amnesia – retrograde and anterograde amnesia.

Retrograde amnesia is when you forget things you knew before the onset of the trauma. Basically, you can't recall old, previously made memories from your past. It can be the loss of memories between just a few hours to many years of your life. For example, you may forget that you are married, that you have children, or that you are a spy who lives under-cover in a country.

Anterograde amnesia is when you are unable to form any new memories after the onset of the trauma. Those who are impacted have difficulty learning anything new. If a person did not already know, for example, that the COVID-19 pandemic broke out in 2020 and that people had to wear masks in public places during lockdowns, it would not matter how many times you tried to tell them, they would not remember this fact anyway. Or say you go together to a restaurant. An hour later, when you ask whether the food was good, the person with anterograde amnesia would not remember that you went to that restaurant or that she or he ate anything at all.

Let's now get back to the discovery of different types of memory. When researchers talk about amnesia, they normally refer to the deficit in explicit memory. It means that an amnesic patient is one who typically has trouble with creating or retaining episodic or semantic memories. They may forget, for example, some well-known facts or they may be unable to recall some past events or even years from their life.

Importantly, the decades of research revealed one interesting fact. At some point, scientists discovered that amnesic patients actually retained some part of their memory abilities (which later became known as implicit memory). Though amnesic patients may not remember who they are, they can retain the skills they already have (e.g. how to get dressed, how to speak) and even learn new tasks and procedures. For example, a professional musician may forget whether or not they own a piano, what type of music they like, or where they studied how to play, but they still know how to play like a pro.

MEMORY DYSFUNCTION

Then some more time passed and more cases were studied. Brain imaging technology (e.g. PET scans, fMRI) became available for diagnostic and research purposes. As a result, it became possible to actually scan what happens in the brain, which significantly advanced research in the field.

First of all, scientists have been able to look more closely at the brain itself and identify the relevant neuroanatomy and localisation of memory. For example, studies showed that brain regions that played the most important role in procedural memory involved the basal ganglia and cerebellum.

According to the brain scans, these brain regions became active once a procedural task was learned or executed. By contrast, some other studies indicated that working memory was dependent on the prefrontal cortex, and so on.

Second, there is now more understanding of the origins of memory dysfunction. Memory problems can be due to brain damage, such as a stroke, tumour or concussion, which can harm any brain region, resulting in problems with movement control, language production, etc. Memory problems can also be due to degenerative diseases such as dementia, Alzheimer's, Parkinson's, etc. Other factors include alcohol abuse, substance abuse, traumatic experiences, depression, ageing, or even too much stress.

In addition, we now know that there are some diseases or conditions that affect only one memory system (e.g. only procedural memory). But there are also diseases (like Alzheimer's, for example) that can disrupt multiple memory systems in the long run.

Alzheimer's disease typically affects the episodic memory system first. The disease damages the hippocampus to a greater extent than other brain regions, which impairs the ability of the person to retain and retrieve new information. But as the pathology of Alzheimer's disease begins to progress, it can affect more widespread areas of the brain. Frequently enough, the patient then develops problems with other explicit types of memory (semantic and working memory).

You can find a brief summary and overview in the table opposite. In the sections that follow, we will consider some interesting case studies from neuroscience to get a better understanding of the topic.

Memory type	Anatomy	Concerns	Commonly associated neuropathology
Working memory	Prefrontal cortex, subcortical structures	Cannot retain new information in mind (e.g. forgetting what needs to be done just after hearing the instructions)	– ADHD – Frontotemporal dementia – Schizophrenia – Alzheimer's disease
Semantic memory	Inferior and lateral temporal lobe	Amnesia: cannot recall well-known facts (e.g. the name of a family member, the number of months in a year)	– Semantic dementia – Alzheimer's disease
Episodic memory	Medial temporal lobe (inc. hippocampus)	Amnesia: cannot remember past events (e.g. eating breakfast this morning)	– Alzheimer's disease – Herpes encephalitis – Korsakoff syndrome
Emotional memory	Amygdala	Cannot acquire conditioned emotional responses (e.g. unable to be afraid of dogs after being attacked)	– Multiple sclerosis – Alzheimer's disease
Procedural verbal memory	Basal ganglia, Broca's region	Has trouble with speech production (e.g. how to pronounce familiar words)	– Expressive aphasia – Apraxia of speech
Procedural memory	Basal ganglia, cerebellum	Cannot remember how to perform habitual behaviours (e.g. how to hold a guitar, how to ride a bike)	– Parkinson's disease – Huntington's disease – Tourette's syndrome

LIVING IN THE PRESENT MOMENT:
The case of H. M.

Henry Molaison (also known as H. M.) is perhaps the most well-known patient in the history of brain science. Henry was born in 1926 in Hartford, Connecticut, and his story begins when he was nine years old.

Henry was playing outside his house one day when he got knocked down by a cyclist. The boy fell to the ground and hit his head. Henry might have lost consciousness for a minute, but he soon got up and went home.

It is unclear whether that accident actually caused any problem, as Henry seemed perfectly normal when he got back home. But soon afterwards, the boy started having epileptic seizures, which got worse and worse over time. He could black out multiple times during the day.

This had a terrible impact on all aspects of his life. For example, Henry dropped out of one school because other children were teasing him. By the age of twenty-seven, he was working on an assembly line, but he had to quit because it was too dangerous for him. So basically Henry had to stay at home all day with his parents.

Henry was given high doses of anti-epileptic medication, but it did not help. In their desperation, Henry's parents sought help from neurosurgeon William Scoville at Hartford Hospital in Connecticut. Scoville and his colleagues examined Henry and tried to identify the part of the brain where his seizures started, so that they could possibly remove it. They said that if they removed some deep-seated structures in Henry's brain which appeared to be the source of his epilepsy, they could quell the seizures. And the family agreed.

On 1 September 1953, Scoville performed a brain operation on Henry and took out a large portion of his medial temporal lobes, including a sea-horselike structure called the hippocampus. It was an experimental operation, as at that time surgeons did not know everything about the functions of specific parts of the brain. Many operations often involved guesswork to some extent.

But it worked. The frequency of seizures reduced significantly – in some years Henry did not have any seizures at all, in other years he might have a few. So, in terms of epilepsy, the operation reached its goal, as the seizures abated. But the procedure, hopeful at best, went terribly wrong in other aspects. Unexpectedly, the surgery left Henry with an extreme memory deficit. After the operation, he was no longer able to establish any long-term memories, which is the condition known as anterograde amnesia.

Up until then, the scientific community did not know that the hippocampus was critical for creating new memories (namely, episodic and semantic memories). And if we lose the hippocampus or have it impaired, we will also lose the ability to store new information. When it was realised, this finding was quickly disseminated so that nobody ever repeated such a procedure.

But it was already too late for Henry. The operation rendered Henry, aged twenty-seven, profoundly and invariably amnesic.

Henry preserved most long-term memories that were created before the operation. His knowledge about the world (semantic memory), for example, was excellent. He could tell you facts about the Second World War, for example, or when the Great Depression started, or name his favourite movie stars. He also preserved many memories of his personal life (episodic memories), though not everything. He could recall, for example, scenes from his childhood, as well as his parents, his classmates, things that he loved to do, such as roller-skating, and many events that happened up until the age of twenty-seven. He also remembered Scoville and their pre-operational discussions.

Yet Henry was unable to form new long-term memories (semantic and episodic ones). He could retain information for around thirty seconds or up to a few minutes through rehearsal in his working memory. But he could not convert these short-term memories into long-term ones.

On 1 September 1953, time basically stopped for Henry. He lived the subsequent fifty-five years of his life, until his death in 2008, in more or less thirty-second intervals. Some would say he lived in a permanent present moment. His personal history was also frozen, as he could not update his memory database. He just experienced every new moment of his daily life – having a chat, reading, walking – as if it happened for the first time.

In practice, this meant that Henry could not learn new facts or words, or form recollections of recent events. He simply forgot all new experiences and information within thirty seconds or so.

Henry did not know, for example, what year it was or who the current president of the US was. He never again clearly remembered where objects he regularly used were kept in the house.

Henry forgot a list of words soon after reading them. Therefore, he could reread the newspaper and magazines without recognising their contents. He could watch the same movie over and over again, and each time with the same wonder and interest.

Henry could also easily forget that he had eaten recently. If you asked him 'Have you had dinner?', he would say 'I don't know', or 'Maybe'.

What's more, Henry was not aware of the passage of time. He grew older, as everybody else did. And though he could recognise his ageing face in the mirror, he did not know how old he was. In Henry's later years, people often asked him how old he thought he was. He always made a series of guesses, saying: 'Thirty?', 'Maybe forty?' When Henry was more than fifty, one of the researchers handed him a mirror and asked: 'What do you think now?' Henry gazed at his reflection, at his elderly face, for a while and replied: 'I'm not a boy.'

In addition, Henry could not recognise a person he had talked to a few minutes earlier. You could meet him, have a conversation, walk out of the room, come back in a few minutes, and you would have to introduce yourself all over again. He would greet you as a stranger and could tell the same story, even with the same vocabulary, having no idea that he had already met you five minutes ago.

A number of hospital staff and researchers spent decades with Henry after the surgery, taking care of him and gathering information about his condition. Of course, they got to know him very well over all those years and even considered him a friend. But Henry did not know the first thing about any of those people. Each of the thousands of times they met, he believed it was the first time they had seen each other.

The saddest thing of all was that Henry did not know whether his parents were still alive. He had a feeling that he was still living at home with his mother but was not sure where his father was. In reality, at that time Henry was living at a nursing home in Connecticut, where he spent the last twenty-eight years of his life, and both of his parents were long gone.

After the disastrous surgery in 1953, Henry was no longer able to live independently. He was looked after by his parents until their death, and then by one of his relatives. And in 1980, Henry moved into the nursing home, where he spent the rest of his life.

If someone told Henry that his parents had already passed away, he would relive the grief over their loss every time he heard about it. At some point he decided to write a note to remind himself that his parents were already dead and carried it for a while. But it was a terrible experience. It is like living in a personal hell in which you find out about the most horrible news over and over again.

No doubt, that condition was a tragedy for Henry. But it was one of those unfortunate cases that unexpectedly turned out to be a scientific breakthrough. For the next fifty-five years, up until his death in 2008, Henry participated in endless experiments, mainly at Massachusetts Institute of Technology (MIT). He sat for brain scans and did different performance tasks. He was a very friendly person and always a pleasure to work with. He never seemed to get bored of all those tests, probably because they always appeared new to him. The access to Henry was carefully restricted. And in publications, he was referred to as H. M. to protect his identity.

Now let's talk about the main discovery. Henry's case revolutionised our understanding of how human memory was organised. One thing that became clear was that there were different memory systems, and these systems resided in different parts of the brain.

Up until then, it was commonly believed that memory was stored throughout the brain. But Henry's case clearly showed that different types of memory rely on specific regions of the brain. In particular, the hippocampus proved to be crucial for creating new semantic and episodic memories.

Moreover, it turned out that Henry was still able to learn new motor skills. In other words, he was still able to form some type of memories on some level – which are known today as procedural memories.

Brenda Milner, a renowned neuropsychologist, did a famous experiment. Henry was supposed to trace a five-pointed star while looking at it in a mirror. It is a moderately tricky task the first time you do it. And, of course, Henry could not do well at first. But he was asked to repeat his efforts. Surprisingly, his performance gradually improved. With repeated trials, it became progressively easier for him to perform this task. Eventually, he became proficient and could trace a complicated figure easily. Milner recalls that after one of the trials Henry said: 'Huh, this was easier than I thought it would be.'

Henry was completely unaware that he'd had training before. But his hands and muscles were learning. He was learning subconsciously.

Clearly, Henry retained the ability to acquire new motor skills. This suggested that there were at least two different memory systems in the brain – one is responsible for conscious, 'episodic' memories, and the second is responsible for skill-related, 'procedural' memories.

And it also meant that these two systems relied on two different brain regions. Henry's hippocampus was largely absent. But if he was still able to learn motor skills, it meant that other brain regions were doing this work.

We now know that procedural memory depends largely on the basal ganglia and cerebellum, which are found in entirely distinct parts of the brain. Since both structures remained intact after the surgery, Henry was still able to build new habits and motor skills.

So far so good? Let's draw on the Pyramid Model to summarise Henry's case. So, we can illustrate Henry's condition as follows:

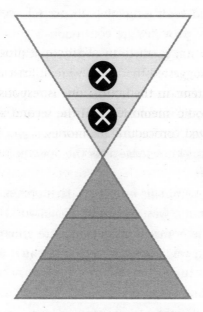

Henry had damage to the hippocampus - as a result,
his semantic and episodic memories were impaired,
but his procedural memory remained functional.

- *Reason (working memory)* – Henry's intellectual abilities, attention, self-control and working memory all remained unaffected. In fact, Henry's IQ was above average. He was as intelligent and able to problem-solve as he was before the surgery. He would often sit doing crossword puzzles, as he believed that this pastime helped him to recall words and retrieve facts from his semantic store. Henry could also maintain information in his mind for several minutes, which indicated that he had proper working memory. He could even remember things for up to fifteen minutes, provided he continuously rehearsed this information in his head and was not distracted.

- *Belief system (semantic memory)* – Henry remembered much of what he had learned prior to the operation. But he was unable to learn new facts, vocabulary or enrich his knowledge after the operation.

- *Memories (episodic memory)* – This system and type of memory was the most impaired. Henry lost many memories of his personal life prior to the surgery and was unable to remember any new events from his life.

- *Emotions (emotional memory)* – Henry was still able to have and express emotions. He was very softly spoken and cheerful, with a great sense of humour, and greeted all strangers as friends.

- *Speech (procedural verbal memory)* – Henry did not have any language deficit. He loved to converse and tell stories.

- *Behaviour (procedural motor memory)* – Henry could not remember the face of a person he had just talked to, but he retained the ability to develop new skills and habits through practice and repetition. He could do everyday things, such as going to the shops with his mother and carrying the bags, making his bed, reading, watching TV or mowing the lawn.

Of course, there are other amnesic patients who have been studied since. But Henry Molaison taught us more about the brain and memory than anybody could expect.

Suzanne Corkin, a neuroscientist who worked with Henry for almost five decades, recalls some very interesting episodes. She used to ask occasionally: 'Henry, you know you are really famous because of all the research that you're helping us with?' He seemed happy to hear that. But, of course, Henry did not know that. No matter how many times people told him that he was famous, he'd forget it in thirty seconds. Corkin also asked Henry about how he was feeling about doing all those tests. After a short pause, Henry would say: 'The way I figure it is, what they find out about me helps them to help other people.'

WHEN IT DOES NOT FEEL SAFE:
The case of a hidden pin

Let's now talk about another famous case, which is related to emotional memory. The case was described by Edouard Claparède, a Swiss neurologist, who studied patients with memory loss.

In 1911, Claparède was treating a patient suffering from anterograde amnesia (the same disorder that H. M had).

The female patient preserved her old long-term memories as well as her reasoning skills, but she could not form any new memories (episodic and semantic ones). For example, she met Claparède on a regular basis, but she had absolutely no recollection of any of these meetings. She did not even remember Claparède's face – so when Claparède greeted her, he had to start with an introduction and other formalities all over again.

Though the woman obviously could not remember recent events, Claparède suspected that she might have some residual memory abilities. He decided to test this possibility with an experiment. Claparède hid a pin between his fingers when the woman arrived the next day. He reached to shake the woman's hand and pricked her with a pin. The poor patient squealed with pain and withdrew her hand, which was a natural reaction. The sharp pin surprised the woman, and she asked the physician to explain himself. But when Claparède left, the woman forgot this incident within a few minutes, as if it never happened.

The following day, however, was an absolute eye-opener. As always, the female patient did not remember the events of the previous day. But when Claparède went to reintroduce himself and extended his hand in the gesture of greeting, the woman refused to shake it. That was very strange. The woman did not remember the doctor, for sure. She did not consciously recollect any prior painful encounter with him. But still, she was reluctant to take his hand.

When asked, the woman could not explain the reason for her refusal; this was obviously a very confusing situation for her as well. But Claparède did not give up and pressed her for an explanation, asking: 'Still, why do you think you don't want to shake hands?' Eventually, the woman gave in and responded: 'Sometimes people hide pins in their hands.'

This devilish experiment showed that, as a matter of fact, Claparède's patient did preserve some memory abilities after all. Even though the poor woman could not consciously recall the original encounter with Claparède, she managed to form some type of memory of this original event. Namely, she could remember at some level the physical pain associated with Claparède's handshake.

We don't know for sure what really happened that day. Since brain imagining technology was not yet available at that time, Claparède could not scan his patient's brain to see the nature and extent of her brain lesions. However, we can make an educated guess. Returning to our explanation of different types of memory, we can assume that Claparède's patient had a problem with the explicit type of memory (episodic and semantic memories), but her implicit memory (in particular, emotional memory) was intact. That's why she was still able to acquire emotional memories and remember the bad experiences, such as a recent painful handshake.

Anyway, this is just conjecture. The real evidence of such a scenario was provided almost ninety years later. Let's consider one very clever and interesting experiment.

In 1995, researchers from the University of Iowa compared three subjects: one with damage to the hippocampus (which is critical for both episodic and semantic memory), one with damage to the amygdala (which is important for emotional memory), and one with damage to both brain structures.

A series of coloured lights was shown to the subjects. But a blue light was always followed by a loud and very unpleasant blast of a horn. The goal was to create a conditioned fear response to a blue light. After repeated trials, a blue light was shown on its own, without any blast, to identify whether the subjects would be afraid of it. After several trials, healthy subjects eventually responded with fear whenever they saw a blue light (as they were afraid to hear the blast of the horn again). Researchers then measured responses of the subjects with brain lesions.

A patient with damage to the hippocampus (explicit memories) failed to acquire any recollection of the situation or knowledge of this experiment, but she did acquire the conditioned fear response. In other words, since her hippocampus was impaired, the subject suffered from amnesia and thus could not acquire any explicit memories. The subject did not remember the experiments, and did not remember the association between the blue slide and the horn. But with the spared amygdala, the patient was still able to form emotional memories. As soon as the blue light was presented, the patient instantly responded with fear, even though she could not understand why.

In fact, Claparède's patient potentially might have suffered from the same condition. The only difference between the two subjects is what they learned to be afraid of. Claparède's patient learned to be afraid of the handshake (which caused physical pain), while the patient from the later experiment learned to be afraid of the blue light (which caused psychological distress).

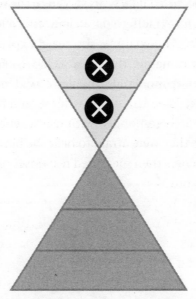

A patient with damage to the hippocampus - as
a result, her semantic and episodic memories are
impaired, but her emotional memory is spared.

By contrast, the patient with damage to the amygdala
(emotional memories) did not acquire a conditioned fear
response to the blue light, but she remembered and understood the situation. It was the opposite to what happened
with the first patient. With the damage to the amygdala,
the subject was unable to learn emotional memories any
more, which would elicit an emotional response, such
as fear. For example, researchers did not detect that the
patient had any physiological arousal to the blue light,
such as an increase in the heart rate. But since other brain
regions were spared, the patient could still remember the

situation, learn neutral facts about the circumstances of the experiment, and explain them. When the subject was asked what happened, for example, she could explain that when the blue light came on, the horn sounded. But again, the subject did not demonstrate any emotional reaction when that happened.

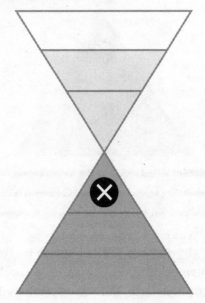

A patient with damage to the amygdala - her
emotional memory is impaired, but her semantic
and episodic memories remain functional.

And lastly, the third patient, with lesions to both amygdala and hippocampus, acquired neither conditioned fear nor any knowledge of the situation. Basically, this patient suffered from the whole pack of issues of the two other patients.

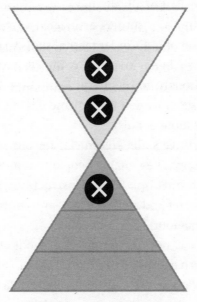

A patient with damage to the hippocampus and amygdala -
semantic, episodic and emotional memory are all impaired.

WHEN THE BRAIN CEO IS OFF:
The case of executive function issues

Now let's consider what happens when people have difficulties with working memory. Have there been times when
you just could not focus on your work? Have you ever found
yourself looking out the window, watching funny videos,
playing games when you were meant to do your duties? With
all the distractions that come our way, we all have trouble
concentrating from time to time. But for some children and
adults, focusing and getting things done is extra hard. They
may have something known as an executive function issue.

Let's define, first of all, what executive function is before analysing issues or disorders associated with it. Executive function is a set of high-order mental skills that help people to control their behaviour and complete tasks. Executive function is thought to involve at least three skills or abilities: working memory, self-control and flexible thinking (see Chapter 5 for more details).

These executive skills are crucial for our normal everyday functioning. They enable people to remember distinct pieces of information, follow instructions, focus, plan, problem-solve, set and achieve goals, and control their emotions and behaviour.

However, it is not uncommon for people to have some difficulties with executive function. This can affect a person in different ways and to a different degree. Basically, any or all of the executive skills mentioned above can be compromised. Some people struggle more with working memory (staying focused, remembering stuff). But others may also have difficulty with self-control (regulating emotions, behaviour, impulses) or flexible thinking (prioritising and planning).

To illustrate, let's meet Chris, a twelve-year-old with an executive functioning issues. He is a smart kid, but he has trouble staying focused and organised. To understand some of the ways that executive functioning issues affect kids and grown-ups, let's take a look at a typical day in Chris's life.

7 a.m.
The alarm goes off with an ear-piercing sound. Chris has a really tough time waking up. 'What time is it? Oh, okay. Still

early. Five more minutes ...' He presses the snooze button and falls back asleep. It feels like five minutes have passed. Chris scrambles for his phone. 'What time is it now?'

8.15. a.m.
'SHOOT: I am late! There is no time for breakfast.'

8.25 a.m.
After brushing his teeth and throwing on clothes, Chris skips downstairs, grabs his backpack and races out to catch a bus. 'I am out the door ... Hold on ... It feels I'm forgetting something ... SHOOT: my lunchbox!' Chris runs back inside, grabs a bag on the kitchen worktop and sprints to the bus stop. The bus is about to pull away ... 'If I miss it, I will have to wait another fifteen minutes ...'

8.40 a.m.
'Woot! On the bus ... I can still make it to my first class ...' While riding the bus, Chris decides to listen to his favourite playlist, but the battery is almost dead. He forgot to charge his phone last night.

9.15 a.m.
'Fifteen minutes late ... Not so terrible ...' Chris tries to listen to his tutor, but it is really hard for him to stay focused. He stares at the board, doing a good job of pretending that he is following the discussion, but he keeps 'spacing out'. At some point, the tutor asks: 'Is everything clear?' Chris gives a thoughtful nod, like everybody else, because he does not want his classmates to think he is stupid.

10.20 a.m.
The tutor asks: 'Who can try to do an assignment related to our new theme?' Chris is terrified, hoping he won't be called on. He's missed half of what the teacher was saying and he has no idea what he is supposed to do.

2.30 p.m.
Bob and Alice, Chris's classmates, suggest going to see a new film in an hour. Chris is thrilled because this a great film, so he checks his calendar. 'SHOOT ... The film overlaps with my football training ... This would be the third time I've skipped training this month ... But I definitely can't miss the film ...' It is hard for Chris to prioritise tasks during the day – he often picks up different projects and then freaks out when he does not have time to finish any of them.

5.30 p.m.
Walking out of the cinema, Chris realises that he left his jacket in the cloakroom. He races back to collect it. 'That was close ... I almost lost my second jacket this year.'

7.45 p.m.
Back home, Chris sits down to do his homework. A book essay is due tomorrow. But it is always a problem to get started. Chris can't work out what to write and only gets a title down on paper. He surfs the web to do some research but ends up checking out funny videos in his social network.

9 p.m.
An hour has gone by and Chris has written almost nothing. 'Okay, I must keep pushing ...' After lots of self-prodding, Chris throws himself into research again. And then he writes and writes and rewrites ... It is getting extremely hard to hold all the thoughts in his mind while working with different information. His mind just keeps jumping from one thought to another.

11.45 p.m.
Chris stays up extra late to finish the essay and almost passes out in front of the laptop.

12.20 a.m.
It is way past Chris's bedtime. But it takes him another hour to fall asleep, as he can't shut off his mind-chatter. Having to burn the midnight oil, Chris got overly stressed and did not have time to wind down before bedtime. Tomorrow is gonna be another rough morning.

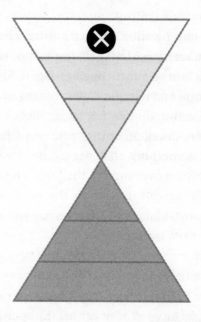

Reason (prefrontal cortex) is unable to properly perform
executive function. A person may experience difficulty with
attention, working memory, self-control, flexible thinking.

It is important to note that trouble with executive function
is not a disorder or a learning disability. There is no diagno-
sis called 'executive function disorder' or 'executive function
issue'. Executive function issue refers just to a weakness in
mental skills that is responsible for difficulties with attention, working memory, self-control or flexible thinking.

It also should be noted that there are many things that
could result in executive function weakness. A common
cause, for example, is ADHD (attention deficit hyperactivity
disorder). ADHD is a biologically based disorder that makes

it hard to focus or control impulses. Kids or adults with ADHD have a chronic difficulty getting organised or staying focused. But apart from ADHD, there are also other causes of executive function weakness, such as depression, dementia, brain injury, and even simple day-to-day stress.

Furthermore, we should not forget about the natural stages of brain development. Strong executive function skills are not something that we are born with. Instead, these skills develop over time as the brain grows. Executive function skills depend mostly on the frontal lobe of the brain – the prefrontal cortex. And the frontal lobe is among the slowest parts of the brain to develop. Executive function skills typically develop most rapidly in early childhood – when kids are between three and five years old. But they are still limited at this time. These skills then continue to develop gradually all the way through school and beyond. In fact, executive function skills are not fully mature until people are around twenty to twenty-five years old.

The point is that it naturally takes time for executive function to develop. And executive function can develop at different rates in different people. That's why some kids with poor executive function may lag behind their peers for a while in school. For the same reason, many of us have turbulent years during adolescence. Teens may still lack the necessary executive skills to control their emotions, to be organised, to consider the consequences of their actions, or to think flexibly when faced with a setback. But as we get older, most people tend to develop better executive skills and experience fewer challenges with it as adults.

Unfortunately, this impulsive or disorganised behaviour

in kids and teens is often misunderstood. It is often assumed that such kids are just being lazy, that they are not very smart, or that they are just incapable of achieving more. But the truth is that it has nothing to do with IQ or behavioural problems. In fact, kids like Chris often try as hard as they can.

There are lots of kids and teens who have temporary issues with executive function during natural brain development. They may try really hard to get organised, or keep their impulses in check, but still struggle socially and academically.

Moreover, it is good to know that there are many adults with ADHD who never outgrow the executive function issue. As grown-ups, they may find it difficult to meet household demands, to manage tasks at work or to sustain attention during a conversation, or they may jump from job to job. Again, it does not mean that they don't try or intentionally want to drive you crazy.

Either way, having support from family, tutors and friends is invaluable. With the right support, kids and adults can work around many of their challenges and thrive at school and work, and in everyday life.

Did you know, for example, that Michael Phelps, the Olympic swimmer, has ADHD? Michael was diagnosed with ADHD at the age of nine. 'I [saw] kids who, we were all in the same class, and the teachers treated them differently than they would treat me,' Michael told *People* magazine. 'I had a teacher tell me that I would never amount to anything and I would never be successful.'

But Michael's mother, Debbie, never gave up on her son.

She established a routine at home, modified his diet (to reduce sugar intake) and introduced him to swimming. Busy schedule, intense exercise, clear rules – these all created a lot of structure in Michael's life. At first, it helped him to be able to focus without medication. And eventually, through practice and dedication, Michael became the most decorated Olympic athlete of all time, with twenty-eight medals in total, including twenty-three gold medals.

FORGETTING HOW TO WALK:
The case of mini-stroke

Walking upright on our two feet is one of the first skills we learn in life. It may be difficult to imagine that a person may forget how to walk if we do this every day. But it might happen – basic motor skills and habits can deteriorate if the procedural memory is impaired.

One common example is when a person suffers a stroke. An individual may lose the ability to perform most automatic, skilled actions, such as how to tie one's shoes, how to eat with a knife and fork, or how to swing a tennis racket.

Here is some good news. When it comes to a stroke and procedural memories, there is the possibility of rehabilitation. If the brain damage is not too severe, people may relearn the lost skills, at least to some extent. In this case, many repetitions of a task need to be performed. Therapists help patients to perform a certain task over and over again, and encourage them to continue practising their exercises at home. With time and practice, task performance improves.

The bad news is that the restored skills may not be as effortless and automatic as they used to be. Even several years after a stroke, a person may still rely on explicit thinking and explicit knowledge to perform simple tasks that most people take for granted.

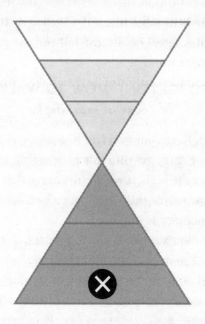

In August 2018, after finishing a daily workout at home, Michael Johnson began to feel unwell. He noticed strange physical sensations in his left side, tingling and numbness in his left arm, lack of co-ordination and weakness in his left leg. Something just didn't feel right. Michael called his wife and described the sensations. Everyone agreed that they should head directly to hospital, just not to take any chances.

It was a wise call. Michael – the legendary US sprinter, four-time Olympic champion, just fifty years old at the time – was having a stroke. At the hospital, doctors diagnosed a transient ischaemic attack, also known as a mini-stroke.

Michael's condition deteriorated rapidly. He was able to get on to the MRI table himself, but when the scan ended thirty minutes later, he almost fell off the table. Michael could no longer walk.

It all looked like a nightmare. Michael Johnson is widely considered as one of the best sprinters of all time. In the 1990s, he dominated 200-metre and 400-metre races. He won four Olympic gold medals, set world records and was virtually undefeated in the 'long' sprints for much of the decade. The fans called him quite simply 'Superman'. And now this: Johnson – the once champion sprinter – could no longer stand.

Anyone in such a situation starts asking difficult questions: Is it possible to recover? Will I be able to dress myself? Will I need others to take care of me? Frustratingly for Johnson, there was no answer to those questions. There was a great team of doctors but the only thing that they could say was: only time will tell.

It is difficult to hear things like that. It made Michael feel scared, wondering what his future was going to look like. Then anger boiled, as he started asking: 'Why did it happen to me, when I was doing all the right things?' Michael was determinedly clean-living – he did not smoke, ate healthily, worked out, kept his weight down – but still ended up having a stroke.

Michael cycled through these emotions until pinpointing one thing that he could possibly control: rehabilitation. Doctors pointed out that the best chance of recovery was to get into physical therapy as soon as possible. That was some relief. Michael quickly shifted into his athlete's mindset, focusing on getting the best training sessions and getting better with each repetition.

The man had to overcome the greatest challenge of his life: going from being the fastest long-sprinter in the world to needing to learn how to walk again. Two days after the stroke, Michael got back out of bed with assistance and went around the hospital with a frame and walker. Ironically, the first walk was about 200 metres – the distance he used to sprint. In Atlanta in 1996, Michael covered 200 metres in 19.32 seconds, breaking the world record. In 2018 in hospital, it took him around fifteen minutes to cover the same distance.

But Michael was determined to run again. With every step he took, he was relearning. He learned how to hold his balance, then how to walk, then how to get up and down stairs. At home, he did therapy twice a day, working on his strengths, power and motor skills.

And it worked. Michael recovered fully and impressively quickly. In less than nine months, he was back to where he was before the stroke. Not only was he back to walking but also sprinting. 'I'm back to running, not as fast as when I was competing in the Olympics but I wasn't running that fast before the stroke either,' Michael said.

THE WALKING BOMBED:
The case of alcohol blackout

Above, I have described quite extreme cases when there is an impairment at one or other level of the mind. But believe it or not, you may experience similar issues even if you are an absolutely healthy person.

Consider the so-called alcohol blackout. Simply put, alcohol blackout is memory loss that occurs after drinking too much alcohol. If you have alcohol blackout, you can't form any new long-term memories, even though you can be still awake and actively interact with your environment. You can talk to your friends, you laugh, you dance. But you are not creating any new memories of these events. Basically, you temporarily suffer from anterograde amnesia at this moment. And when you wake up the next morning, you have a vague or no memory at all of what happened last night.

Here is a possible example from a day-to-day life. Imagine that you drank too much at a holiday party. The next morning you wake up and you barely remember what happened last night. But it turns out that you managed to get home on your own somehow. You walked, took a cab, opened the door and crawled to the bed.

What actually happened that night in your brain? On the one hand, alcohol affected those regions of the brain that are responsible for your recollections (episodic and semantic memories). That is why you failed to encode new information and thus don't remember well the details of last night.

Alcohol also affected your reason system. As a result, it became much harder for you to control your actions – even simply to co-ordinate your moves. It also became difficult for you to do any complex high-level mental activity, such as thinking clearly, paying attention to what other people say, or making rational choices. That is why, when we are drunk, we are so silly and do all those things that we would never do when we're sober – like dancing on the bar or making out with a girl or guy you just met.

But not everything is so bad. On the other hand, that night alcohol did not affect those regions of the brain that are related to your habits (procedural memory). Thus, despite the fact that you were intoxicated, you were still able to fall back on your habits and successfully get home on autopilot, as you usually do.

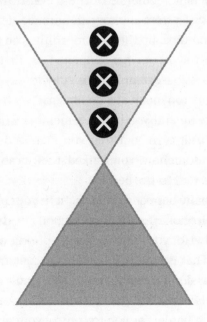

THE BRAIN COMPENSATORY MECHANISM

Our mind consists of multiple memory systems, and they are relatively independent. In some sense, this helps us not to keep all our eggs in one basket. This means that if one system of your mind is out of service for some reason, other systems can remain functional. Should any of the systems founder, other systems can remain intact and come to your rescue.

Consider, for example, the alcohol blackout case again. When intoxicated, you may fail to memorise new information and use executive function well (think critically, control behaviour, regulate emotions). Nonetheless, you can still fall back on your habits and get home safely.

——————— Chapter summary ———————

- Amnesia is the inability to form new memories, recall old ones, or both.
- Retrograde amnesia refers to the inability to access old memories (episodic or semantic memories).
- Anterograde amnesia refers to the inability to create new memories (episodic or semantic memories). A person with this type of amnesia can forget such things as a phone conversation five minutes ago, that they had cereal for breakfast today, or whether they turned off the oven. Any event that happened today will not be recalled tomorrow.

- If one system of the mind is impaired (either temporarily or permanently), other systems can remain intact. It is often the case that if explicit types of memory are impaired, implicit types of memory remain functional, and vice versa.

4

The Training Plan

Train Like a Mixed Martial Artist

SOME THOUGHTS ON
PERSONAL CHANGE

The long-term memory is being filled continuously from our early childhood. From the very day we are born, we constantly take in new information – from what other people say, what we read in books, things we watch on TV, and any other external influence we are exposed to. We thus gradually obtain firm beliefs about ourselves and about the surrounding world, we build habits and acquire experiences, which all stick with us into adulthood.

One problem here is that a lot of our 'programs' are installed in early childhood, when our ability to reason is still limited. The mind of a child is wide open, to absorb any information from those who surround them, including limiting beliefs, unhealthy habits, irrational fears and traumatic experiences. Ultimately, we do not choose most of our programs in the first place and are left to deal with them on our own as grown-ups.

But don't worry, change is possible. In fact, it is possible to make changes at each level of the mind to further our health, performance and sense of happiness. For example, we can break bad habits, such as smoking or waking up late, and build much better and healthy habits, such as eating vegetables or working out regularly. We can change negative beliefs about ourselves or about life and replace them with more positive alternatives. With some effort, we can get rid of phobias and become much more confident and stress-resistant. We can even change how we remember things, making our bad memories, for example, much more neutral and less distressing.

It is not an easy task, for sure. Most of these programs exist for years, creating a certain comfort zone for us. Therefore, whenever you want to change something or try something completely new, it naturally causes emotional and even physical discomfort.

That said, it is definitely within your grasp to program and re-program your mind, at least to some extent. Otherwise, psychotherapy or such things as personal development simply would not exist.

In this context, it is useful to get back to the concept of memory, which we have discussed thoroughly in the previous chapters. Knowing the nature of different types of memory is one of the most important *keys to change*. Changing your habits (procedural memory), for example, will require time and consistency. To change your negative beliefs about yourself or the world (semantic memory), you will need to know how to identify false assumptions in your thinking. At the same time, if you want to work with your recollections (episodic memory) or phobias (emotional memories), you will need the knowledge of how to deal with intense emotions, and so on. In each case, we will need a unique approach and a toolkit.

More on how to actually make a change and manage your mind is in Part Two and Part Three. We will consider each level of the Pyramid Model individually and learn how to work with them.

THE MIXED APPROACH TO PERSONAL MASTERY

If you have read the Introduction, you will know that I represent the 'integrative tradition' in psychotherapy, which underpins my approach to personal development. If you have skipped that part, I encourage you to go back, as it will help you to better understand the context and motivation behind this book.

Here is a quick recap. While a student, I was studying psychotherapy and martial arts side by side. Eventually, I ended up favouring the mixed approach in those two fields, rather than strictly adhering to any pure style or school. I simply could not ignore the fact that other schools could offer many effective methods and techniques (either in fighting or treatment). Plus, the big idea was that as you diversify and enlarge your arsenal of techniques, you also become much more prepared to deal with a vast number of situations.

I hope it sheds some light on the context. And you won't be left wondering what on earth prompted me to use combat sport metaphors in a book that should explain how to achieve more inner peace and happiness.

MMA CURRICULUM

Speaking of integrative self-care, I like referring to MMA (mixed martial arts) as a helpful analogy. Let me backtrack a little and quickly explain what the MMA curriculum entails. After that, we will move on to integrative self-care and consider our mental health plan.

Even though MMA is a blend of different styles, it does not mean that MMA is a chaotic style. There is actually a very clear structure behind this combat style. In particular, it is common to break down MMA's skill set into *three core components*: stand-up fighting, clinch fighting and ground fighting.

Stand-up fighting, as the name suggests, is a fight between opponents in a standing position. It typically includes punches, kicks, and knee and elbow moves. For example, the most common martial arts that focus on stand-up fighting are boxing, karate and kickboxing.

Clinch fighting is when opponents are engaged in the clinch (stand-up grappling). It typically entails clinch holds, kneeing, takedowns and throws (to take an opponent to the ground from a standing position). For example, styles that are well known for clinch fighting are sambo and judo.

Lastly, ground fighting is a fight between opponents that takes place on the ground. It consists of strikes from the ground-based position, grappling manoeuvres and submissions. For example, you can find a lot of ground fighting in Greco-Roman wrestling and Brazilian jujitsu.

In essence, these three components cover all possible aspects of the fight. Many people will be at a loss, for example, when they are taken down to the ground. But it does not matter much for an MMA athlete. They are equally skilled in the stand-up, clinch and ground game. So, even on the ground, there are many wonderful options for how to win a fight.

Basically, that's a common ground. Every MMA fighter will have to train in these three disciplines to be successful in the sport. You may be a professional wrestler who knows how to do stunning takedowns, even have an Olympic medal, like Ronda Rousey,* for example, but if you don't have the necessary skill sets in the other two aspects of fighting, you won't get far in MMA.

The athletes differ, however, in their choice of techniques and background. For example, some MMA practitioners may focus just on boxing to improve their stand-up fighting, while others may prefer drawing on muay thai and capoeira. Still others may come with a strong base in taekwondo, and so on. This is what makes the style of each fighter unique and unpredictable.

---

* Ronda Rousey is a mixed martial artist and professional wrestler. Rousey started pursuing a career in MMA after winning an Olympic bronze medal in judo at the 2008 Summer Olympics.

INTEGRATIVE THERAPY CURRICULUM

While integrative therapists seek to combine different approaches, it does not imply that the integrative approach is simply a mishmash of different methods, nor that the therapy does not have any structure, or that the integrative therapists just randomly pick what they feel would work. If you work with an experienced therapist, they are trained to combine techniques based on specific principles and frameworks, so your sessions won't feel too loose or experimental.

So what is the structure behind the integrative approach? I won't be speaking here on behalf of every integrative specialist, because there are different views and approaches to integrative therapy. But the way I see it, at the very least, an average integrative therapist is trained to deal with multiple aspects, dimensions or layers of mental health.

The term 'integrative' refers not only to bringing together different approaches to help you. 'Integrative' also refers to pulling together different layers or components that make up your mental wellbeing.

Typically, if a therapist practises an integrative approach, he or she will consider, at least, *three* major layers of their client's functioning – namely, cognitive, affective (emotional) and behavioural levels. In other words, they are trained to work with thoughts, emotions and behaviour. That's the minimum, as a rule.

However, it is also common to go a bit further sometimes. Some integrative therapists also take into account, for example, physiological and social levels. In this case, a therapist will pay attention to how you feel physically and examine social aspects of your life (e.g. your relationships, upbringing, how your environment and cultural norms affect you, etc.).*

Basically, integrative therapy aims to *promote healing on all levels* – to ensure that all levels of a person's functioning (i.e. cognitive, emotional, behavioural) are looked after and maximised to their full potential.

In fact, it is very easy to draw a parallel with MMA. To be successful in a fight, you need to cover all aspects of combat – namely, stand-up fighting, clinching and the ground game. The integrative approach is based on the very same principle. To be good at self-care or psychotherapy, you need to cover all aspects that are crucial for mental wellbeing – in particular, at least, cognition, emotions and behaviour.

And the techniques that you can use to manage each of those dimensions are limitless. For example, you may get strategies from CBT to get better at managing your thoughts. There are many cognitive techniques that are likely to be very helpful. But if it does not work so well for you today or tomorrow, or it does not work for your clients, you can always try something else.

---

* I do also consider physical and social levels, as a rule. Though these levels are very important, without any doubt, I tend to treat these levels as complementary, compared with the levels related to our mind. That's why I don't mention them in this book. Perhaps I will focus on these complementary levels in other work.

THE TRAINING PROGRAMME

The training programme suggested in this book will include the work with the six levels of the Pyramid Model. As you can see in the table below, there is a specific goal that we will try to achieve at each of the levels.

Levels	Training goal
1. Reason	Developing mindfulness
2. Beliefs	Managing thoughts
3. Memories	Managing memories
4. Emotions	Regulating emotions
5. Speech	Creating supportive stories
6. Behaviour	Building healthy habits.

In Parts Two and Three, each chapter has the same structure. Each includes three simple and effective techniques that you can do in order, all at once, or at separate times, to reach one of the training goals.

COMPATIBILITY WITH OTHER APPROACHES

It should be noted that major schools of psychotherapy work exactly on these six themes or levels of mental health. I don't want to make an exhaustive comparative analysis, as this is not an academic manuscript. Overleaf, you can find just a snapshot of what some therapies do and focus on.

Theme	Description	Therapy example
1. Reason	Mindfulness-based interventions apply meditative practices and teach a person to cultivate mindfulness (focus their attention on their thoughts and feelings in a non-judgemental way).	Mindfulness-based cognitive therapy (MBCT)
2. Beliefs	Cognitive therapies primarily help a person to explore and change the way they think.	Cognitive behavioural therapy (CBT)
3. Memories	The psychodynamic approach traditionally pays much attention to our past experiences. It helps a client to get insight into how their past experiences affect their current behaviour.	Psychodynamic therapies
4. Emotions	Almost all types of therapy address emotions one way or another. But some therapies place emotions front and centre during therapy sessions.	Emotion-focused therapy (EFT)
5. Speech	Speech therapy is mainly about how we sound. It addresses speech disorders and helps to improve communication skills. Meanwhile, therapies such as narrative therapy focus on what we say. It will lead the client to create and tell more positive stories about their life.	Narrative therapy
6. Behaviour	Behavioural therapy seeks to identify and change problematic behaviours.	Exposure therapy

The Pyramid Model is not a theory of everything. But, as an integrative framework, it bridges the gap between many major approaches to self-care. To put it differently, it is compatible with many major approaches at the same time. For example, if you've been a big fan of cognitive therapies, such as CBT, you will still be able to work with your thoughts and even use the same techniques that are common for CBT.

But more importantly, you then have a choice. You can either restrict yourself just to the cognitive level, for instance, if you want to or if you believe it is sufficient. Or you can go a little bit further. You can go up and work on your mindfulness skills, for example. Or you can go down and work with your past experiences, or with your habits, or with any other level that requires attention and care.

THE PREMISE

In essence, our strategic goal is to promote healing on all levels. Potentially, if one of those six areas of the mind is neglected, your overall wellbeing and performance could be diminished. For example, it is important to know how to challenge your negative thoughts, as they can result in anxiety, low self-esteem and even depression. But it is not enough. It is equally important to know how to cope with your painful memories, as they can haunt you for years and even decades, frustrating you and putting you down. In addition, it is also useful to know how to break bad habits, as they can systematically undermine your health and per-formance. The same is true for the other levels.

At the same time, if you take care of each level of your mind, this can potentially have a huge positive impact on your health and life success overall. The point is that while each part of the mind plays an independent and important role in our wellbeing, if we attend to all six areas of the mind, we create the *synergy* that can radically transform our health, boost daily performance and significantly improve the quality of our life.

All in all, the plan is that by the end of this training programme you will become a well-rounded self-care practitioner. Well, at the very least, I will do my best to help you with this enterprise, in our metaphorical MMA self-care gym. So, put your gloves on because our training is about to begin.

--------- **Chapter summary** ---------

- Memory is relatively resistant to change. For this reason, it is often hard to change ourselves, and change always takes time. You can't, for example, talk yourself out of having a habit or having a phobia.
- Nonetheless, change is possible. If needed, you can revise the deep-seated programs of your mind. For example, you can consciously question the truth of your beliefs, revise your habits, and so on.
- One of the premises of the integrative approach is that all aspects or dimensions of mental health are important.
- Therefore, integrative therapists tend to promote

healing on multiple levels: emotional, cognitive, behavioural, physical, etc.

- It is suggested that it is important to keep all levels in check to achieve optimal functioning and wellbeing.

Part One

Visual summary

Levels of the Pyramid Model	Types of memory

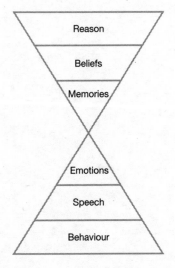
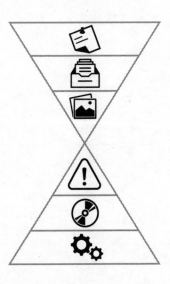

(Working, semantic, episodic, emotional, verbal procedural and motor procedural memory)

THE TRAINING PLAN

Levels	Training goal
1. Reason	Developing mindfulness
2. Beliefs	Managing thoughts
3. Memories	Managing memories
4. Emotions	Regulating emotions
5. Speech	Creating supportive stories
6. Behaviour	Building healthy habits.

Part Two

The Top Pyramid

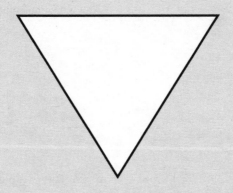

5

Master of Attention

The chief executive officer (or CEO) is the highest-ranking position in an organisation. The CEO is responsible for making key managerial decisions and leading a company to success. Whether you've ever been a senior leader or not in the business world, there is actually a region in your brain that is responsible for executive function.

You can think of the reason system (or the prefrontal cortex) as the management system, the executive system, or simply as the 'CEO' of the brain. The prefrontal cortex is the region of the brain that sits just behind the forehead. It is one of the last areas of the brain to develop, fully maturing at around the age of twenty-five. And it is also the part of the brain that is necessary for skills that are essential to adults, such as focusing attention, controlling impulses, good judgement, setting goals, problem-solving, decision-making, and so on.

Overall, the prefrontal cortex is thought to fulfil the so-called 'executive function'. Executive function has come to be an umbrella term for diverse high-level mental skills and abilities that help us to get things done. Not all researchers look at the executive function in the same way. But many understand it as a group of important skills that include paying attention, working memory, flexible thinking and self-control.

Executive function skills	What it means	Examples
Attentional control	The ability to pay, sustain and shift attention.	– concentrating on a task at hand and ignoring distractions (e.g. listening to a lecturer, reading a book, fixing a car, playing a video game) – searching for your flight on a departure board – checking a business letter for mistakes – drawing straight lines in a diagram – turning around when you hear someone calling your name.
Working memory	The ability to retain information in the mind and work with it over a short period of time.	– holding on to information you've just read – recalling the name of your first teacher (retrieving information from long-term memory).

Executive function skills	What it means	Examples
Flexible thinking	The ability to problem-solve, plan, think of something from multiple angles.	– considering answers to a quiz question – comparing two products before making a purchase – solving a maths problem in two different ways – adjusting plans when something unexpected happens.
Self-control	The ability to control behaviour (initiate, guide, monitor), inhibit impulses and regulate your emotions.	– forcing yourself to run another mile, when your body is already tired and sending signals to take a break – turning the wheel slowly and carefully when learning to drive – not overreacting when faced with criticism – not blurting out inappropriate things during business negotiations – resisting eating a piece of chocolate cake in the evening – stopping yourself from engaging in risky behaviours.

Each of these executive function skills plays its own independent and important role. But they also work in conjunction with one another. As a result, we are enabled to self-regulate and manage daily tasks successfully.

When people have a problem with executive function, it affects them in all aspects of life – at home, school, work and social life. Such individuals find it hard to stay focused, handle emotions, regulate behaviour and accomplish long-term goals. We've already discussed the so-called 'executive function issue' earlier in this book (see Chapter 3). It is now time to consider what can be done to strengthen and develop our executive potential.

Let's start with the question: 'How can we detect the activity of the conscious mind?' As a rule of thumb, all operations of the conscious mind require *focused attention*. Take a look again at the examples listed above. Focused attention is necessary for each of the above-mentioned activities. You need to stay focused when you hold information in your mind and try not to forget something. You also need to pay close attention whenever you actively think of something. And you need to keep focused whenever you guide and control your behaviour. If you're distracted, and your attention is drawn away, then you will perform much worse.

As you can see, the ability to pay attention is an absolutely fundamental skill. More importantly, it is one of those skills that can be developed and improved. Even if you don't have any attention problems, there is no doubt that you can significantly benefit from strategies designed to improve your focus and ability to be present.

COMMON PROBLEM:
Zoning out

I bet you've heard lots of times the phrase 'live in the present'. But do you really understand what it means? Aren't we all in the present now? Well, physically, yes. But mentally, we can be far away from the present moment.

The great role of the conscious mind is that it helps us to notice or register the things that happen around us right now. And whenever we go on autopilot, we space out. Yes, we do understand what we are doing at this moment – you realise, for example, that you're taking a shower and not walking to the grocery shop. But on the whole, your aware-ness can be far away from the present moment. You can be deep down in your thoughts, daydreaming about a new car, planning your week, and so on.

Why do we zone out? I'd say that the first reason is biological. The mind needs to process a large volume of information each second, and it often diverts our attention from the present moment into other mental processes. You may, for example, get caught by some rambling thoughts. You may self-analyse or pass judgements on things that have happened recently. Or you may indulge in fantasies. Thus, we can be mentally checked out most of the time.

The second reason for zoning out is, probably, related to technology and the modern way of life. As members of an informational society, we are constantly bombarded by a vast amount of new information and stimuli, as never before in human history. To put it bluntly, new generations grow up with a habit of seeking new stimuli all the time. We scroll on our phones, check our messages, respond to posts, and so on. Consequently, nowadays people are arguably less accustomed to concentrating on just one thing. Most of us just get bored instantly if we don't get our usual level of stimulation.

That said, mind-wandering isn't all bad. It is actually a normal part of how our brain works. In the automatic mode, we are able to make plans, think of how to deal with different situations, look for creative solutions, access what happens around us, etc. So, even though we may zone out from time to time, we may still do lots of things in this state that can be very helpful and actually crucial for normal everyday functioning and survival.

But while there are some benefits of mind-wandering, there are also many downsides. As a matter of fact, it all depends on when and how often you zone out. The problem begins when zoning out seeps into areas of your life that require forethought and being present here and now, such as communication with other people, learning, taking business decisions, spending time with your loved ones, etc.

Overall, if we start to favour automaticity, we take less conscious control of our behaviour, which can negatively affect our performance and wellbeing. There are some good reasons to want to stop zoning out too often. Let's take a gander at a short list.

- *Missing the now* – When mindful, we are aware of various aspects of life, both the good and bad. But if we switch to autopilot, we are not really connected to the world around us. As a result, we miss out on multiple things that happen around us in the present moment. For example, you may miss what other people tell you in a conversation and have to ask them to repeat it. Or you can suddenly realise that you have no idea what you've just read and need to back up a page to find the last point you followed.

- *Missing the good moments* – Sadly, as we go through our days on autopilot, we rarely notice the beauty and wonders that the present moment may offer. To illustrate this, consider the 'violinist in the metro' experiment. In 2007, Joshua Bell, one of the best violinists in the world, posed as a street musician and played for free at a Washington D. C. subway station. Joshua played for around forty-five minutes on a violin worth $3.5 million. As it was rush hour, thousands of people went through the station. But how many of them stayed to appreciate the performance? During the forty-five minutes, only seven individuals stopped for a while and listened to Joshua playing. The rest were rushing to meet their schedules, without stopping for a minute.

- *Mindless decision-making and mistakes* – For the same reasons, we are also prone to making mistakes in our decisions and behaviour. As we tune out, we take action without stopping to think about what we are doing and how we are doing it – which can sometimes lead to trivial slips, costly blunders at work, or even dangers to life. Take driving home as an example. Believe it or not, according to statistics, most car accidents happen near home. The thing is that when the route gets familiar and habitual, we become less attentive to it. Thus, we may neglect to check the traffic before stepping out into the road or forget to check the mirrors when driving out of the petrol station.

- *Forgetting* – As we zone out, we also tend to become more forgetful. Have you ever intended to grab a bottle of milk or some other product in a grocery store on the way home but forgot? This can be explained by the fact that awareness plays an important role in the memorisation process. When we are absent-minded, we are really bad at encoding new information. That's why, whenever we slip into autopilot, we then have a hard time recalling the details of certain recent events and or even how we behaved. As an example, do you often remember your morning drive to work? To be honest, sometimes it can be a total blackout time. You may remember how you leave home, how you arrive at work, but not the trip itself. By the same token, you may quickly forget the name of the person you just met. Or you may barely remember some 'little things', such as what TV programme you watched a few days ago or where you put your car keys. Or you may doubt whether you closed the door or turned off the hob in the morning.

- *Feeling that time flies* – Have you ever felt that weeks and months fly by? In this auto-state, we also experience time passing much faster. In fact, time flows at the same pace when we are children and adults. The only thing that differs is whether we are present or not. If you go on autopilot, you do not register the present moment well, so it feels that time passes by very quickly. That's why, rushing from one appointment to another, we may suddenly realise that the year has almost zipped by. At one point, you may blink and then boom! Here you are celebrating another New Year, sadly looking back and wondering where all the days, months and years went. Where the heck did the time go?

TRAINING GOAL:
Developing mindfulness

The opposite of being zoned out is being mindful. Mindfulness is an ancient concept that has its roots in Buddhism. Buddha included mindfulness as one of the steps in the Noble Eightfold Path, the teaching towards nirvana and enlightenment. Yet today, mindfulness meditation is available as a totally secular practice. It is being actively applied in a variety of fields, including education, sports, business and even the military. Moreover, increasingly, therapeutic schools are including meditation as part of their treatment plan.

So what is mindfulness? There is still no universally agreed definition of this term in psychology. But I don't think that we will be far off the mark if we define mindfulness as follows: mindfulness is the ability to pay attention to the present moment, without judgement. Let's break it down.

Ability to pay attention	This means that you direct attention to what is happening right now, instead of getting lost in your thoughts. No zoning out, no autopilot. You pay attention only to what you are doing, hearing, feeling, or seeing in the present moment.
Non-judgemental attitude	This implies paying attention to everything that happens now - thoughts, feelings, events - without judging them. You don't comment on what is going on, nor do you attach any labels, such as 'right' or 'wrong', 'good' or 'bad', and so on. You just observe the events in an open, curious and non-judgemental way.

You may wonder: are mindfulness and meditation the same thing? These two terms are often used interchangeably, with little explanation of either, which adds to the confusion. The short answer is 'no'. Mindfulness and meditation are not the same. I suppose it is helpful to draw a clear line between these two concepts.

The two can be described in just a couple of words: mindfulness is a state of mind; meditation is a practice. Mindfulness is the ability to be present – to be aware or conscious of the things that happen right now (without judgement). By contrast, meditation is a practice or activity. It is a thing you do. There are many types of meditation, such as sitting meditation, walking meditation, kindness meditation, body scan meditation, and so on.

Another important point is that meditation, as a practice, helps to develop many qualities, such as kindness, compassion, a tranquil state of mind, etc. And, among other things, meditation may help to develop mindfulness. In other words, if you meditate, you can train yourself to be more mindful – to be present and less distracted. By analogy, if meditation is like working out or going to a gym, mindfulness is more like strength or endurance that you develop after training sessions.

The main question is: why train yourself to be more mindful? According to available studies, it looks like mindfulness can produce a positive effect basically on every single system of the brain and body. It is suggested that its benefits include:

- enhanced psychological health (reduced symptoms of anxiety, depression, stress, pain, mind-chatter)
- improved general physical health (e.g. better sleep, lower blood pressure)
- improved cognitive functioning (e.g. self-awareness, lengthened attention span, decreased age-related memory loss)
- increased happiness and life-satisfaction.

To be fair, robust research on mindfulness is only in its infancy. Much more research is needed to conclude what cases can be well addressed by mindfulness and meditation practice. Nonetheless, there is little doubt that you can reap benefits from developing the state of present-moment awareness.

PRACTICE #1:
Come back again and again

This first practice is meant to form the right attitude to your wandering mind. It is a very important step before you can move on to any meditation practice itself. It is akin to learning how to make a fist before throwing any punches, because if you don't form it in a proper way, you may end up breaking your hand.

One common misunderstanding is that meditation is about making your mind go blank. Or a related myth is that mindfulness is a state of having no thoughts.

The problem, however, is that the mind doesn't tend to stay still. If you meditate, for example, and try to focus your attention just on one thing, such as your breath, you will find that at some point your attention will leave your breath and wander to other places. You may start rehashing some stressful situations from your day, for instance, or plan what you have to do at work tomorrow.

In fact, the belief that one needs to empty one's mind is often the reason why many people give up before they get any experience or benefits from meditation. It is very easy to get frustrated by your wandering mind. I remember feeling very annoyed with myself when my mind did not stay in one place during my first meditation sessions. It looked like I was doing it all wrong, as I believed that you truly meditate when you have a constant state of laser-like, present-moment focus.

The good news is that you don't actually need to make your mind go blank. While meditation does often lead to a quieting of the mind, it does not mean that you are supposed to empty your mind or become free of thoughts. Normally, meditation means being able to focus your attention, to become aware that your mind has wandered away, and then bring your attention back. Here are some ideas for how to make friends with your mind-wandering, rather than treating it as a mistake or failure.

First of all, you should recognise that it is a natural condition for minds to wander. Instead of the term 'mind-wandering', you can use the term 'think in automatic mode'. And there is nothing wrong with this – it is okay to have thoughts come and go. It is simply what minds do. To be more exact, it is what the belief system does. The belief system is designed to process information and generate thoughts in automatic mode (see Chapter 6 for more details). And the belief system does this work non-stop, whether it is while meditating or going about daily life.

It is almost impossible to switch off this automatic thought process. Even if you've managed to meditate for seven straight days, you will still get thoughts flash in your mind every ten seconds or so. In fact, if the belief system did stop doing what it is supposed to do for some reason – such as planning, analysing, daydreaming – it would be a huge problem for your normal everyday functioning and survival. So let's be grateful for its valuable work.

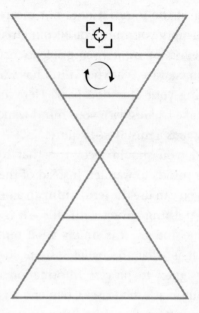

While the reason system puts effort into concentrating
on something, the belief system generates automatic
thoughts and processes information in automatic mode.

Second, it may seem surprising but mind-wandering is
actually an important part of mindfulness and meditation
practice. Moreover, paradoxically, being distracted from
time to time is what helps to build focus. Let me explain.

Put most simply, meditation is a way to train your attention to stay in the present moment (rather than following
your thoughts into the past or future). Meditation involves
choosing a focus for your attention, such as the sensation of
your breath, and bringing your attention back every time it
wanders. Note the second part of that definition – 'bringing

146

your attention back every time it wanders'. If we had to summarise the main stages of mindfulness and meditation practice, it would look something like this:

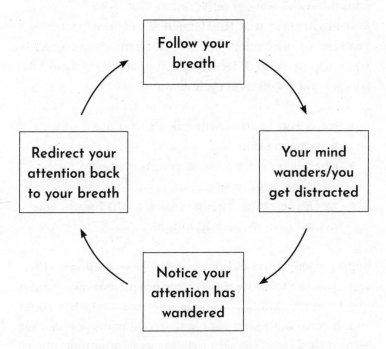

So there is a very predictable cycle. During a basic meditation session, you are instructed to focus your attention on a single object, usually your breath. It seems like a very simple task to do, but it is much easier said than done. Give it a try for a few minutes and see what happens. It will not be long before you start thinking of something unrelated to what you're doing. At some point, you might realise that your focus is no longer on the breath at all. With this awareness, you can stop yourself from following thoughts and bring your attention back to your breath. But don't think that you have managed to tame your mind. After a few breaths, the cycle is likely to repeat. Sooner or later (probably sooner), your mind will wander off again.

It might seem that this tendency to get distracted is a problem for meditation. But, in reality, mind-wandering is what helps to train different aspects of attention. Let's take a look at the meditation cycle again:

- when you focus on the breath, you use a skill to sustain attention
- when you notice a wandering thought, you use a skill to detect distractions
- when you return attention back to the breath, you use a skill to redirect attention.

Suppose your mind did not wander. How would you then train yourself to notice that you are not present? How would you hone the skill to bring your attention back? You could not. It turns out that it is only when thoughts pop up that we can fully build the skill to control our attention.

Let's recap. The first thing that we've learned is that it is natural for the mind to wander. Some levels of the mind simply work in automatic mode and need to process volumes of incoming information every single second. So let's be grateful for its valuable work. Second, it is even helpful to have thoughts come and go during the meditation practice. You may get distracted from time to time, which, of course, can feel frustrating. But, more importantly, you also learn to recognise the moments of being distracted and learn to steer your attention back to your breath. Therefore, you are still training and gradually improving your attention span.

So don't worry if you don't manage to clear you mind of all thoughts. That's okay. Whether we are meditating, driving somewhere, cooking, having a conversation, we all get absorbed with a thought occasionally. It is something that will always happen. The goal is just to recognise when this happens and bring your attention back again and again.

PRACTICE #2:
Five senses exercise

It is always good to have some anchors that can help us to bring attention back to the present moment. One of the basic anchors that most people have at their disposal all the time is one of our five senses – touch, smell, hearing, sight and taste.

The five senses are your gateway into the present moment. That's because only your senses really know the present, what happens here and now. You can't taste the future or touch the past, for example. Your senses can pick up only what happens right now. This stands in stark contrast to your fantasies, thoughts or memories, which make your mind time-travel, taking you either to the future or to the past.

So if you want to reconnect with the present, one of the easiest ways to do that is to tune in to one of your five senses. Whichever of the five you choose to engage, it will allow you to get out of your head and reconnect with the present moment.

This exercise is a great entry point to mindfulness practices. It is quick, simple to learn and easy to do. It takes only a few minutes to tune in and scan what is going on around you. Importantly, you can do it anywhere, whether it be in bed, in your office, in the coffee shop or during a walk.

As you start the practice, you will be amazed at how many things have gone unnoticed in your life. You will discover more tastes, hear more sounds, see more details.

Below is a simple sequence to guide you through how to tap into your five senses. All that is needed is to notice what you're experiencing with one of your five senses in this exact moment, without judgement.

Directions

1. *Relax* – Find a moment when you won't be disturbed or interrupted. Take a few deep and relaxing breaths.

2. *Tune in* – Engage one of your five senses for at least a minute. Just pay attention to what you experience (see, hear, smell, touch or taste), without judgement. Pick a sense that works best for you right now. Below are some examples of how you can kick off:

Sight
Bring your attention to what you can see in the surrounding environment. Pick any object that you normally don't notice and focus on its visual

details. It could be the shape, the texture, the colours, the shades, changes in light, movements. Try not to label, analyse or judge what you see as good or bad. Just observe.

Hearing

Start to tune in to what you hear around you. Open yourself up to all the sounds in the background and notice subtle things that you normally don't register. It could be things like the faint rustle of leaves on a tree, the chirp of a bird outside, the noise of traffic from a nearby road, water dripping, the hum of the fridge, or the beats and tunes of the songs in your playlist. Try not to judge or comment on what you hear. Just listen.

Smell

Take a moment to notice the smells and scents of your environment. Try to catch any subtle smells that you usually filter out. Does the air smell hot or cold? Does it smell clean or fresh? Perhaps you might catch a whiff of baked pizza from a local Italian restaurant or a waft of freshly cut grass. Do you pick up a scent of perfume, flowers or salty ocean? Maybe a coffee aroma? Try not to judge the smells as pleasant or unpleasant. Just catch the scent.

Touch

Shift your attention to the things that you're currently feeling. It could be the feeling of pressure of your feet on the ground, the smooth surface of a table under your arms, the fabric of your clothing against your skin, the breeze across your face, the temperature, like warmth or coolness, or water on your body as you take a shower. Try not to get caught in any commentary or analysis of what you feel. Just notice the sensations.

Taste

Move your attention to the sense of taste within your mouth. For a start, just run your tongue over your teeth and cheeks and notice the current taste in your mouth. Alternatively, take a sip of drink or take a small bite of some snack. Then bring your awareness to the taste, all the flavours and textures that arise, such as sweetness, bitterness and the aftertaste. Try not to judge the food as good or bad. Just stay with the taste.

PRACTICE #3:
Focused-attention meditation

There are plenty of meditation techniques that can promote mindfulness. Here, we will take a look at one of the most basic ones, which is known as focused-attention (FA) meditation. If you are a beginner at meditation, focused-attention meditation will be a good starting point. It is a relatively easy practice to learn and to do. In addition, this form of meditation has been studied scientifically and proved to generate many benefits for its practitioners.

When you practise focused-attention meditation, not only do you train your attention to stay in the present moment (instead of wandering off with thoughts in the past or future and worrying about everything), you also gradually cultivate a calm and focused state of mind. With time, this can yield profound results, reducing mind-chatter, stress and making room for clarity and kindness.

Focused-attention meditation is exactly what is sounds like. The participants are instructed to focus their full attention on a single, chosen object. Unlike trance – where your attention is dispersed – with focused-attention meditation you learn to concentrate and sustain your attention on one thing, most commonly the experience of your breath, a calming sound, a smell or some external physical object. And when your mind wanders, you are asked to bring your attention back to a chosen focal point.

The goal is neither to think about the process of breathing nor to control it. The idea is simply to observe and experience it. Bring your awareness to where the air goes when it enters and leaves your body. Feel how your lungs fill with air. Note how your belly gently rises and falls as you breathe. Notice how your diaphragm (the muscle below the lungs) moves. Zero in on the quality of each breath: whether it is fast or slow, deep or shallow, the time between the breaths.

Also, it is important to note that this practice is not about sitting with an empty mind. Sooner or later, your mind will inevitably start to wander off to other places. It is more about realising that you are off track and bringing your attention back again and again.

Instructions

1. *Get settled* – Pick a quiet, comfortable place where you won't be disturbed. It is not necessary to fold your legs into a lotus position. Just find a comfortable position where your body is relaxed but spine is upright, without being too tight or rigid. Legs can be crossed if you sit on the floor; if you sit on a chair, make sure your feet touch the ground. Close your eyes to reduce visual distractions. Notice your body as you sit still.

2. *Focus on your breath* – Gently bring your full, undivided attention to the experience of your breath. You don't need to try to control your breath – making it deeper, longer or shorter. Just notice the natural rhythm of your breath – in and out. See if you can feel the sensations of breath as they occur. Maybe you can feel how cold air flows into your nostrils as you inhale, how it goes out of your mouth as you exhale, how your belly moves.

3. *Bring attention back* – At some point, you may notice your mind start to wander from your breath. You may start thinking of other things or getting lost in memories. That's perfectly normal. When you notice that your mind has wandered, gently return your attention back to your breathing. After a few breaths, the mind will wander off again. Once again, take note and gently bring your attention back to your breathing.

4. *Avoid judgements* – Do you remember that mindfulness involves the non-judgemental attitude? Let go of any judgements during the practice – e.g. judging whether you're doing it right or wrong, whether you achieved anything, etc. Just observe.

5. *Finish the session* – When you are ready – after five, ten, thirty minutes – take three deep breaths and gently open your eyes. Notice how you feel after the practice. You can begin with short meditation sessions (e.g. two or five minutes) and then gradually increase the length (ten, fifteen, thirty minutes). You can work your way up to longer sessions once it gets easy and comfortable enough.

Visual summary

Common problem:
Zoning out

Training goal:
Mindfulness

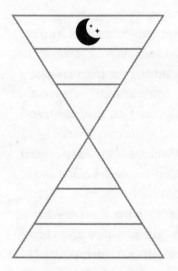

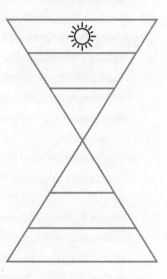

─────── **Chapter summary** ───────

- The reason system performs the so-called executive function in the brain. Executive function skills typically include attention, flexible thinking, self-control and working memory.

- Attention appears to be essential for all executive function skills. Attention is the ability to focus on one or few things.

- Meditation is a practice that trains your attention.

- Mindfulness is the ability to pay attention to the present moment, without judgement – be it a walk in a park, the mere act of breathing, or the sound of a favourite song.

- When you start to meditate, you will come up against the tendency to space out and run away from the experience of being in the present moment. You may start rehashing some stressful situations from your day or plan what you have to do at work tomorrow.

- Many people falsely believe that they need to make their mind go blank. And with that end in view, they set about controlling their mind during meditation sessions by trying to stop thinking or to force any thoughts out. As a rule, these attempts fall short and the mind keeps racing.

- If you find your thoughts drifting a lot, that's okay. That's what our mind does. It is natural for our mind to stay active and wander away from time to time.

- The purpose of meditation is not to get rid of thoughts and sit with an empty mind. Rather, it is about recognising that your attention has been distracted and bringing it back to your breath repeatedly.

- As a first step, it would be useful just to notice and get to know when you zone out. You can simply make a mental note: 'Hey, I've just zoned out.'

6

Master of Thoughts

The belief system is primarily responsible for two things – it stores our beliefs and generates automatic thoughts. Let me break it down for you.

First off, the belief system is home to our semantic memory. In the broadest sense, it stores all our beliefs and knowledge of the world (see Chapter 2). Think of it as a big filing system for your mind. For example, it stores beliefs about yourself (e.g. your name, date of birth, what you like or dislike); beliefs about other people (e.g. biography of your parents, understanding who is your best friend, etc.); beliefs about the world (e.g. that a year consists of twelve months, cooking recipes, understanding when it is safe to cross the street, etc.).

But that's not all. In addition, the belief system also generates so-called automatic thoughts.* Automatic thoughts are subconscious, habitual and instantaneous thoughts that

---

* The term 'automatic thoughts' is widely used in cognitive therapy, in particular in CBT.

occur in response to everyday events. They come to mind automatically. They just pop up or flash into your head without a conscious intent or effort. Have you ever been doing something, like scrolling on your phone, folding laundry or driving to work, when some random thought just sprang into your mind, as if from nowhere? That's an automatic thought.

You may wonder what the relationship is between beliefs (semantic memory) and automatic thoughts. I want to clarify this point straight away, before we move any further.

In short: automatic thoughts are the products of the beliefs we have. Throughout life, we acquire beliefs about the world, about ourselves, and then those beliefs interpret the events that happen around us, giving rise to our automatic thoughts.

Picture this situation: a girl named Alice came to believe in her childhood that to be attractive, she must be skinny. Then, let's imagine that Alice put on some weight during the summer holiday. One day, she looks at herself in the mirror and almost instantly hears something like: *Oh my God, I look horrible!* That's an automatic thought. Alice did not mean to think badly of herself. The thought just popped up in her head automatically. The reason is simple. Whether Alice is aware or not, she holds the deep-seated belief that she should always be skinny. This belief, in turn, gives rise to any of those automatic thoughts or personal comments about her looks.

Typically, we experience automatic thoughts in the form of self-talk or mental images. You may hear a verbal thought, such as *It looks like it's started raining again*; or

Damn, I forgot to call my bank manager; or *The floor is slippery. I should be careful*. If you baked a pie and took it out of the oven, your inner voice might say: *Oh my, it smells so good*.

Alternatively, it is also common to experience automatic thoughts in the form of mental images. Many of us are visual thinkers – those who tend to think in pictures. You may involuntarily visualise, for example, that you win a major sports championship and become very popular. Or you may have a sudden picture of your face going red and embarrassing yourself during a presentation at work.

In essence, the belief system is one of the structures that helps you think (subconsciously). But unlike the reason system, the belief system is designed to process information, and to interpret and evaluate events, in *automatic mode*. A typical example could be seeing a car in the street and understanding that it is a car. Or opening a window and quickly judging that the weather is great today. You don't think consciously or intentionally about these things. The thoughts just occur on their own.

Here is another example. Right now – as I am writing this sentence – I'm receiving the inputs from both my conscious and unconscious cognition. On one level, I engage my conscious mind (the reason system) to complete this paragraph. I am thinking of how to complete this sentence, what to write next, and how to do it better. My whole attention is directed at this task only. But on another, deeper level, there are also lots of things that are done automatically. I understand, for example, that I am sitting in my living room; that it is morning now; that it is sunny today; that the funny noise I hear behind my back is made by my dog, probably 'punishing' one of his toys after our morning walk; and that it will be good to take a break after finishing this paragraph and have a nice cup of black tea.

If you pay attention, you will notice that you have the so-called self-talk or mental chatter in the background of your head. Self-talk is an inner dialogue that you have with yourself that can range from making observations about different situations or commenting on your behaviour to thinking of complex tasks or issues. In essence, self-talk is the endless stream of automatic thoughts that runs through your head.

We all have that little voice in the background that seems to have a say on everything that happens around us. It runs almost 24/7. It 'chats' with us throughout the day, commenting on what happens in our lives, what it means, what went wrong, what needs to be done, etc. Sometimes it does not shut up even when we want to take a rest, keeping us awake at night.

However, believe it or not, your mind is not trying to drive you crazy. Instead, it is simply trying to process the available information and make sense of it as best as possible. As we go about our daily lives, we are constantly taking in new stimuli and information from our environment. In turn, your mind is built to process or to digest this never-ending flow of information to make sense of the world around us and to understand the situations you find yourself in. That's why it never stops thinking and judging.

COMMON PROBLEM:
Negative self-talk

If you look at the content of your self-talk, you will quickly recognise that not all of your thoughts are the same. Some thoughts can arise from reason and logic. Some other thoughts can come from misconceptions or lack of knowledge. So they can be inaccurate, biased or plain wrong, even though they may seem rational to us.

The reality is that many of our automatic thoughts are often negative. Negative self-talk is exactly what it sounds like – talking to yourself in a negative or critical way. You may be thinking, for example, about what went wrong, what could go wrong, what you do wrong, or what everybody else is doing wrong.

For instance, if you've got stuck in a traffic jam and are late for an important meeting, your inner voice might say something like: *You dummy, you should've left home earlier.* If the business meeting then did not go so smoothly, you might hear something like: *It is your fault.*

The fact that we have negative thoughts sometimes is not a problem. There is a view that we evolved to think mostly negative thoughts rather than positive ones. Earlier in human history, our ancestors were exposed to constant threats in the jungle. So scanning the environment for potential threats, such as predators, for example, was literally a matter of life and death. Those who were more attuned to danger and were better prepared for the worst had better chances of survival. For this reason, we may be hardwired for negativity today.

Anyhow, if you have negative thoughts on and off during the day, there is nothing to be concerned about. Those thoughts just fly by quickly, not causing much discomfort.

The problem is when your negative self-talk spins out of control, and you start to experience excessive negativity. Sometimes you may get stuck in interpreting stressful events in an overly negative way that keeps going until you become emotionally overwhelmed.

If you've ever found yourself going about your daily life while your mind constantly bombards you with negative thoughts and you jump from one negative feeling to the next, then you know what I am talking about. It can be described as falling into a downward thought spiral.

Negative self-talk can take many forms. It often picks out little things we don't like about ourselves (the flaws that nobody else would even notice). For example, we may beat ourselves up with phrases such as: *I'm a failure, I'm so unlucky, I'm not good looking enough, I am so out of shape, My goals are out of reach, My life is a mess.* Sometimes the voice tells you that some terrible thing might happen. For example: *What if my girlfriend/boyfriend meets someone who is good-looking?, What if I lose my job?, What if I get sick?*

It will perhaps come as no surprise that being caught in a negative spiral can take a toll on your mental health. Of course, the longer the spiral goes on, the worse you feel. For example, if you're in the habit of constantly telling yourself, for example, *I'm unlovable* or *I'm unattractive*, you will find yourself feeling sad, anxious or even depressed. You may also get sick often because, as you experience negative emotions, your brain pumps out a dose of stress hormones that make your body feel bad. You may also find it hard to stay focused and get work done in time, as you experience low energy.

In addition, negative spirals can also block you from living a fulfilled life. Picture this: you'd like to take a trip to Bali and learn to surf. This has been a dream of yours for a while. But suddenly you start having the following thoughts: *I've heard that surfers are sometimes attacked by sharks ... A wave wipeout can leave a surfer with serious injuries ... Bali is so far away ... The ticket will probably be so expensive ... The jetlag might be horrible – I will spend just a week adapting and recovering ... The traffic on the island is terrible ...* In a second, you are overwhelmed with anxiety. And in a minute, you close a browser tab that lists availability at surfing hotels.

If you find yourself at the bottom of a thought spiral, it can be hard to get out of it. Sometimes, the stronger you try to stop the troubling thoughts, the stronger those thoughts become. But don't worry, there are techniques that can help to break the cycle of negative thought.

TRAINING GOAL:
Think realistically

Much of the advice around overcoming negative self-talk is connected to positive thinking. Our generation is obsessed with becoming happy and more positive. Countless books, podcasts and self-help gurus suggest, for example, that you should purposefully focus on the positive or repeat positive affirmations to yourself. For sure, it may work for some people or in some cases. Being positive is a great thing – and you should absolutely try to approach different situations and unpleasantness in a more optimistic way.

However, positive thinking doesn't always work. It is usually really hard to override negative thoughts with more positive ones, if you actually think that some of your negative thoughts are true. You may recite positive self-statements like *I am confident* and *I am strong* every day for hours. But if you hold a deeply ingrained belief that you are *not good enough*, your mind will eventually drift back to old, repetitive, negative thoughts that undermine your self-esteem.

By contrast, when it comes to combating negative thoughts, and to thought management overall, I'd recommend starting with realistic thinking. Rather than forcing yourself to be more positive, we will explore how to examine a negative thought critically, how to undermine its credibility and then how to replace it with a more balanced or realistic alternative.

Let's clarify what realistic thinking is all about. If we view thinking as a continuum, then we have negative thinking on one end of the spectrum, with positive thinking on the other end, and at the midpoint we have realistic thinking.

Optimists, those with positive thinking, are generally those who focus on the bright side of things and expect the best outcomes, being confident that events in one's life will eventually turn out well. Pessimists, on the other hand, those with negative thoughts, are those who dwell on the worst aspects of a situation and expect bad things to happen. Realists, in the meantime, fall somewhere in the middle of the optimism–pessimism continuum. Realists are those who recognise life events as they really are (which can be negative, positive or neutral) and are prepared to deal with them accordingly.

Realistic thinking is based on facts, evidence and logic. Hence, before reaching a conclusion, a realist tends to analyse the question thoroughly and to try to understand the entire situation – both its positive and negative parts, both pros and cons, arguments for and against. For example, when you plan and set future goals, you can ask yourself: 'Is it actually achievable?', 'How likely is it that things could turn out wrong?', 'What can I do to mitigate the risks?', 'Okay, if things go wrong, this is what I can do as a Plan B'.

Realistic thinking involves looking at things – yourself, others, life, the future – in a balanced way, without being overly negative or positive. You try to be honest with yourself, even if a situation looks ugly. You can recognise, for example, that you don't have infinite control over your life or that you don't have the gift of foreknowledge. You can accept the fact that the world is often a cruel and unfair place.

But it is not a type of thinking meant merely to make us look at a situation clearly. It is meant to motivate you to take action and make some real changes in your life. While you can recognise the limitations of the world and yourself, on the other side of the coin you can also actively reflect on the opportunities for improvement. If you've failed a driving test, for example, instead of convincing yourself that you were simply unlucky with an examiner and that you actually drive like a pro, you may agree that there might be a gap in your knowledge or skills, but with practice you can improve on your results. As William Arthur Ward once said: 'The pessimist complains about the wind; the optimist expects it to change; the realist adjusts the sails.'

And here is the best part. There is evidence that being realistic is the best way to achieve long-term wellbeing. In one longitudinal study, researchers examined whether it was pessimists, optimists or realists who had the greatest long-term wellbeing. To test this question, researchers from the University of Bath and the London School of Economics tracked 1,601 individuals over eighteen years.

As part of the study, the participants reported whether they had positive, negative or realistic expectations when it came to their finances. Pessimists, for example, expected to be worse off the following year than they actually were (their financial situation, in fact, did not change). Optimists expected to be better off the next year than they were (their income either did not change or was lower the following year). And realists were those whose expectations in the previous year matched their financial situation the next year.

The researchers followed the participants' actual financial situation and measured how their expectations stacked up against reality. Alongside this, the participants reported on their life-satisfaction and psychological distress. The study found that realists – those who estimated accurately their financial outcomes – had a higher sense of wellbeing than optimists and pessimists.

Why does this result arise? Why pessimists are the worst off in this study is perhaps obvious. They have a gloomy outlook at the outset, which does not allow them to enjoy their victories for long. But why do optimists experience more distress than realists? The researchers suggest that it is possible that for optimists the feeling of disappointment gradually overpowers positive feelings. If you expect much, but don't get it, you will feel like a failure, which, in turn, can generate distress and lead to a drop in a sense of wellbeing.

Of course, there are many factors that contribute to our long-term wellbeing. But it seems intuitively right that making sound decisions based on facts can have a major impact on your health and life satisfaction.

PRACTICE #1:
Monitor

We all have this ongoing monologue in the back of our heads. It never stops interpreting and evaluating events. But since it happens automatically and quickly, we often forget that it is there. Some people even disregard that their inner monologue is mostly critical.

If you want to change how you think or take some control over your thoughts in general, then it is important to recognise what you think in the first place. If we ignore our thoughts or view them as totally accurate, then there isn't much we can do to change them.

For a start, all it takes is to pay attention to what is going through your mind. Take a pause and listen to your mental chatter. How is your 'thought life' looking right now? Are there any disturbing thoughts? The goal right now is simply to become aware of your self-talk.

The good news is that there is no need to keep track of

all your thoughts during the day. There are literally thousands of automatic thoughts that run through your mind every single minute. Noticing all of them would be simply daunting and exhausting.

Instead, it is more practical to track how you are feeling. If you notice a sudden change in how you are feeling, it is a good clue that you have thought about something in a certain way before that. After noticing a negative emotion, you can work back to the level of your thoughts and consider what is going through your mind.

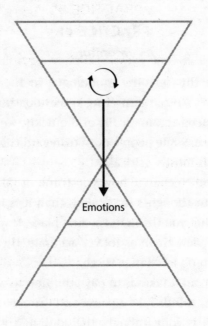

Thinking and feelings are interconnected. Automatic thoughts can trigger negative emotions.

So the plan of action is very simple. If you notice an unpleasant feeling, pause and ask yourself: 'What is running through my mind right now?'

Example: Emma found out that her colleagues went out to the pub the other day but did not invite her. She then noticed feeling very low and sad soon after that. In that moment Emma asked herself: 'What is going through my mind?' She was able to catch some of the following thoughts: *They don't like me, What is wrong with me?*

PRACTICE #2:
Thought record

Whatever it is that goes through your mind and evokes strong feelings, it would be a good idea to write it down. In this case, the best tool at your disposal is to keep a thought record.

A thought record, or a thought diary, is a place where you collect all information related to your troubling thoughts. Thought records are widely used in cognitive therapy, and help clients to identify, evaluate and revise any negative thoughts.

Thought records work best when they are filled in close to the event. The best time to fill the columns is shortly after you notice a change in how you are feeling. Since the episode is still fresh in your mind, you can record as many details as possible. Plus, the faster you reframe your thoughts, the faster you will be able to feel better.

Completing a thought record may seem like a lot of work in the beginning. But it gets much easier with practice. At some point, you will spend no more than a minute or two to fill in the form. More importantly, it is definitely worthwhile and gives a good starting point for changing how you think.

In essence, the purpose of a thought record is to get you into the habit of capturing troublesome thoughts and clarifying their origin and consequences. Simply put, journaling ensures that you won't forget or disregard whatever bothers you. There are lots of people who can spot that they have a troubling thought but do nothing about it. As a result, those unhelpful thoughts can play on repeat for months and even years.

With a thought record, however, you will be able not only to capture what runs through your mind but also keep track of any thought patterns. You may recognise, for example, that your thoughts can be grouped into several big themes. Those thoughts may emerge regularly and cause most of your distress.

In addition, it will be much easier for you to analyse and challenge a thought when it is written down on paper. Trying to keep everything in mind is not the best idea. As you will remember, there are limits to how many things the working memory can hold.

In its simplest form, a thought record consists of a form with four columns to record a) the date the thought happened; b) the situation in which the thought occurred; c) how it made you feel; d) information about the thought itself.

a) Date	When did it happen? Enter the date and approximate time.
b) Situation	What was the situation (when the thought came up)? Where was it? What were you doing? Who was involved?
c) Emotion/body sensations	What did you experience as this situation happened? What emotion did you feel (e.g. anger, sadness, happiness)? What did you sense in your body?
d) Thought	What were you thinking as this situation happened? What went through your mind during or just after the situation? What images popped up in your mind? What did you say to yourself?

Example

Date	Situation	Emotion/ body sensation	Thought
Thursday, 6 p.m.	At work: my boss said that I might take charge of another team next month.	Anxious, stressed, increased heart rate, tense.	I am going to mess up and will be fired.
...	At work - I did not know an answer to my boss's question at a meeting.	Low, tearful.	I made a fool of myself. It is unlikely that I will be promoted.

Date	Situation	Emotion/ body sensation	Thought
...	I texted Alice to ask how she was doing, but she did not respond.	Irritated, sad.	That's very rude. What have I done? She doesn't like me any more.

PRACTICE #3:
Challenge

After capturing a troublesome thought, it is essential to challenge it, where possible, and replace it with a rational alternative.

It is important to remember that our thoughts cannot be considered as a completely accurate source of information. Our beliefs are often based on false assumptions. They are frequently skewed and biased. So it is essential to stop from time to time and examine critically how accurate your thoughts actually are, and whether you are being fair with yourself and others.

Probably, the best way to test the accuracy of your thought is to look at the evidence behind it. To do that, we need to pose a few challenging questions and then do some research. Here are some questions to ask yourself:

- What is the evidence for this thought?
- What is the evidence against this thought?
- What can I do to resolve this problem? If a problem

is real, what can I do to mitigate the risks or resolve the issue?

One helpful way to challenge a thought is to think that you are in an imaginary court case. 'Putting thoughts on trial' is a popular technique used in CBT. Here is how it works. An original disturbing thought is put on trial. The defence is arguing that this thought is true, and the prosecution is arguing that the thought is false. Your role is to be the defence, prosecution, the jury or the judge at the same time. This way you can investigate a situation from multiple angles. You will dismiss emotions or assumptions and stick just to the facts. After hearing all the evidence presented, you can issue a verdict – a balanced and realistic judgement.

The beauty of this technique is that it helps to deconstruct a thought, examining whether our arguments are actually sound or sufficient, and looking at a situation from multiple perspectives in a fair and rational way. Frequently enough, it turns out that the original thought is just irrational, having little or no real evidence to back it up.

Yes, it may take some time to shift a negative thought this way. But I can say with certainty that this approach definitely works and is actively used in therapy. In most cases, you can truly undermine a thought only when you determine that it does not have much ground to stand on. Once you recognise that the thought is not as convincing as it might initially seem, you will be able to dislodge it quickly.

Directions

1. *The dock* – First, put your thought in the dock. Name a negative thought that has been troubling you.

2. *The defence* – Then adopt the role of the defence barrister and identify all the evidence that supports the thought. List all the reasons why you think that the thought may be true.

3. *The prosecution* – Once the defence has presented its evidence, adopt the role of the prosecution barrister and gather the evidence that undermines the credibility of the thought. Come up with all possible arguments why the thought may be false.

4. *The judge's verdict* – Once the evidence for and against the thought has been presented, adopt the role of the judge or the jury to weigh up all the evidence and give a verdict. Given all of the evidence presented, what do you think of the situation and the original thought now? Is there a new, more balanced and realistic way of looking at the situation? Sum up the alternative thought.

5. *An appeal* – Let's assume that you've reviewed the evidence for and against the thought and

still believe that the negative thought is true. If you still think that your original thought is too convincing, continue the disputing process. Try to find more evidence against the troubling thought. Pose more challenging questions, read professional literature, go and talk to people who can share an expert opinion on the matter. Like any good lawyer, you need to do your homework.

Example

Thoughts	Evidence for	Evidence against	Verdict
I am going to mess this up and will be fired.	I don't have strong enough skills to do this work perfectly.	I performed well with the smaller scope of work.	Even though it feels scary, I may learn to cope with more responsibilities and do it well eventually.
I made a fool of myself. It is unlikely that I will be promoted.	My boss seemed dissatisfied that I could not respond.	I performed well multiple times. My boss praised my work before.	It is unlikely that one unfortunate episode could destroy everything.

THE PYRAMID MIND

Thoughts	Evidence for	Evidence against	Verdict
She doesn't like me any more.	She did not respond to my message.	She may have been very busy and then simply forgot, without any intent to offend me.	I can text her again some time and ask whether everything is okay.

Visual summary

Common problem:
Negative self-talk

Training goal:
Think realistically

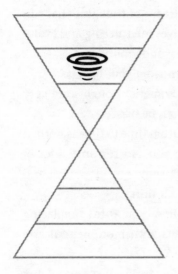 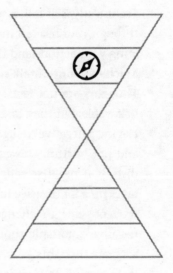

―――――――― **Chapter summary** ――――――

- The belief system is home to our subconscious thinking, which is quick, automatic and often happens unnoticed.
- Automatic thoughts are thoughts that people routinely have during the day and help to make sense of their experiences.
- Self-talk is an ongoing dialogue you have with yourself. Technically, self-talk is a stream of thoughts that run through your head. It involves interpreting and evaluating your actions and the world around you.
- Much of your self-talk stems from your beliefs.
- Thoughts are not facts. Automatic thoughts are very believable, but they can often be biased.
- Having a negative thought from time to time is normal and not hurtful. However, you can run into a lot of distress if negative self-talk spins out of control and takes up a lot of space in your mind.
- It is possible to change how you think, replacing negative automatic thoughts with more helpful and accurate thoughts.
- It is useful to cultivate realistic thinking. Being realistic is a sweet spot between pessimism and extreme optimism.

7

Master of Memories

Episodic memory is the memory of specific events or episodes from our personal past. It gives us the ability to recall situations and details associated with them – be it time, place, people and experienced emotions. A typical example would be remembering your last summer holiday. When needed, you can mentally relive this episode: the places you visited, the events that took place, the people you met, and even how it felt.

In this section, I want to give more details about the nature of episodic memories. Understanding how episodic memories are organised will then help us to work with them. Just as a preview, I will say straight away that episodic memories have two important features: a) they can contain emotions and b) they have a rather malleable nature (and therefore can be changed). Let me explain these two points one by one.

First of all, episodic memory is closely related to our emotions. When we experience an event, the brain can record not only the details of the event itself (the time, the context, what happened) but also the emotions that we experience during that episode.

Physiologically, emotional arousal releases stress hormones that foster the development of new synaptic connections and consolidate new memories. In some sense, emotions 'burn' new memories in your brain.

Have you ever watched Pixar's film *Inside Out*? Even though it is a cartoon for kids, it provides a very clever analogy of how this brain mechanism works. The events are mostly set inside the mind of an eleven-year-old girl named Riley. Within her mind, we can see the personifications of five basic emotions – Joy, Anger, Fear, Disgust and Sadness – that live in 'Headquarters' (a.k.a. the amygdala, the emotional centre of the brain). By pushing buttons on the control panel, the emotions influence everything that Riley does, thinks, and even how she remembers things. Memories are shown as glowing coloured orbs, and each orb represents a specific event in Riley's life. The colour of the orb matches the emotion that dominated during this time: yellow for Joy, red for Anger, green for Disgust, purple for Fear, and blue for Sadness. Orbs are manufactured in Headquarters by Emotions, and then they are sent to the 'Long Term', a library with endless shelves that contain Riley's memories (episodic memory).

In fact, this mechanism makes sense from an evolutionary standpoint. Apparently, we need to prioritise events that were stimulating or significant in some way. If we remember well those things that proved to be dangerous, risky, pleasant or joyful, for example, we can recognise similar things faster in the future. And if we recognise and respond faster to dangerous things, trying to avoid them or taking necessary precautions, we increase our chances of survival.

Can you still remember your first kiss? The surprise birthday party thrown by your friends? What about the time you landed your first job? The time you made an embarrassing faux pas in front of your boss? How about your wedding day? It is a good bet that you can still conjure up many specific details: what the guests wore that day, what the weather was like, how the flowers smelled, what kind of music played, how the cake tasted.

The opposite also holds true. Dull or mundane things are much easier to forget. This is because we don't attach any special significance to them. As Riley's imaginary friend Bing Bong wisely points out: 'When Riley doesn't care about memories, they fade.'

The second important feature of episodic memories is that episodic memories have quite a malleable nature (and therefore these memories can be changed). Let's elaborate on this point.

Subjectively, we tend to experience memories of events like short videos that play back before our eyes. Because we tend to experience memories this way, there are many misconceptions about how memory actually works.

There is a common belief, for example, that episodic memory works something like a video recording. You just record the experience and then play it back. To be more exact, you record the events exactly as they appear in the environment, then you store this video or memory indefinitely, and later on you can play it back intact over and over again, each time reproducing the same order of events. In other words, it is tempting to think that memories of events are fixed and unchanging.

However, that's not how it works. Contrary to popular belief, memories are far from perfect recordings of the past. In fact, memories are highly malleable or plastic constructs. To put it differently, memories are constantly changing. Unknown to the individual, memories are often updated, influenced, easily distorted and forgotten.

There are many theories and explanations as to why our memories are so malleable. One plausible reason is because there is simply too much information to take in. There is an enormous number of sensory stimuli available at any given moment. And our brain is simply not designed to either detect, process or store so much data.

On the one hand, we are unable to notice absolutely everything that happens right now in our environment. The perception system is not built to register so much sensory stimuli. That is why we may sometimes overlook obvious things that take place right in front of us. I don't know about you, but sometimes I catch myself opening a fridge a few times in a row, missing 'something tasty' that is right in front of my nose. There are many experiments that reveal this phenomenon of selective attention or perceptual blindness, if you are interested in the subject. To keep it short, the point is that even if we witness an event, it does not mean that we register all the details about it.

On the other hand, we are also unable to store so much information. Even if you create a vivid and detailed memory of an event, unbeknown to you, the details of this memory may easily fade away with the passage of time – within the next hour, month or even years.

Here, the story takes an unexpected twist. Since we don't

take in everything through our senses and don't store all the details indefinitely, naturally there can be gaps in our recollections. Even if it feels subjectively that our memories are complete, as a matter of fact they are often full of holes.

For example, try to recall your last conversation on a phone. You can probably remember when it happened, who you spoke to, the subject of the conversation, the core message, maybe some key words or phrases. However, it is unlikely that you can recall the whole conversation, word for word. So there are already some gaps in this memory. And after a while, more details of this conversation may fade away, even to the point of completely forgetting it happened.

So where does that leave us? Presented with incomplete information, our brain seeks ways to fill in the gaps. When we don't have all the details, we are inclined to fill in the blanks in our memories to create a coherent story of what happened.

There are many ways in which we can fill in the missing spaces in our memories. In general, people are apt to use whatever information is available at the moment of recalling an event.

First, we may fill in the gaps using our current knowledge as well as our beliefs or expectations. In other words, we can fill in the blanks in the memories with the facts that we assume to be correct, or based on what we know about the world right now. Suppose, for example, you can't remember exactly who was present at your birthday party five years ago. But your knowledge suggests that your best friend Neil always comes to such events. So you may easily add Neil to the memory of that event (even though Neil was, in fact, abroad at that time and could not physically attend your party).

Second, to fill in the blanks in our memories, we often pick up information from external sources – from what other people say, what we read from the news, and so on. Imagine you witnessed a car accident, for example. It happened very quickly, but you saw the moment of the crash. Then you discuss this episode with two other individuals who were standing next to you when it happened. After that, you are questioned by a police officer. And finally you read about this 'horrible car crash' in the news the next day. Interestingly, after all those conversations with different people, your memory of this event may become a blend of a) what you actually saw, b) what you heard from other people about what they witnessed, c) what kind of questions you heard from the police officer, and d) what you read in the news about what supposedly happened.

Let's pause for a moment and recap. So, we don't tend to retain every single detail of a situation. We may unwittingly skip or forget some details over time. Because of this, there are naturally gaps or blanks in our memories. In turn, we are prone to fill in those gaps to make our memories complete (or to make our stories coherent), drawing on our current knowledge, opinions, expectations, or information from external sources.

So what do we have as a result? Basically, every time we fill in the blanks in our memories, we change them. As we insert additional or new information from the present, we update an original memory.

It should be noted that a memory can be changed or updated multiple times. It is not that you have only one attempt. In effect, every time you revisit a memory of some past event, that memory has the potential to change (at least slightly). With each remembering, you may unwittingly insert into your recollection things from the present, such as your current beliefs, feelings, information learned after the original event. If this happens, you basically unwittingly update your memory with the new experience or even rewrite the past with the new information.

So as you can see, our memories do not function like video recordings. In fact, a memory is often a blend of an original event and new experiences. A more helpful metaphor is that our memory is more like a video collage, pieced together from different clips, which sometimes have no relation to the original event. Importantly, this is a video file that you can both watch as well as edit. Every time you open the file, you can always change it a bit, adding, deleting or altering a video sequence.

At first sight, the fact that memory has a malleable nature may make it seem defective or disingenuous. But in evolutionary terms, it makes perfect sense. First and foremost, remembering everything would be simply exhausting. Just imagine how many 'mental servers' you would require, and how much energy these data centres would use to store every single bit of information about every tiny event and experience that took place in your life. So when we remember only a part of the experience, we actually save lots of energy and mental resources.

And to be fair, in reality, there is rarely a need to remember everything exactly the way it happened, with every minute detail. Rather, it seems to be more adaptive to store only that information that is likely to be the most useful in the future.

The take-home message is: memories are malleable, not fixed in stone. On the one hand, this fact is really bad news for judges and juries. In a court room, it would be much more useful to have a video recording or a video-like memory. Unfortunately, our memories of events are not as reliable as we think they are, often containing errors and inaccuracies, which we don't even realise. In fact, false memories are one of the primary causes of false convictions. A false conviction is when a person falsely identifies a suspect, which often happens because of false recollections.

But when it comes to mental health, the fact that memories have a flexible nature is fantastic news. It gives us an opportunity to change the way we remember the past (at least to a certain extent) and make space for a brighter future. If you have a memory that brings you down, you can try to tap into it, expand its content and update the way you remember this episode.

It is often assumed that there is very little that we can do about our past. It is one of the reasons why many people try to avoid their harrowing memories, trying to put their past behind them. However, sometimes it may be more productive to actively recall what is crippling you and work with it, rather than trying to sever the connections with it. Even if you've always remembered an event as being distressing, it is never too late to reinterpret, for example, some aspects of that situation, and reprocess how you remember that event.

I should make it clear that the goal of changing memories is not to fool yourself. We are not going to manipulate the facts behind your memories. If you did not get a job offer, for example, we are not going to pretend that you actually did.

Or if you went through a highly distressing or painful event, we are not going to pretend that it was in fact satisfying.

Instead, the point is to know how to reprocess old memories so that they build you up and benefit you instead of holding you back or tearing you down. Minimally, we will try to learn how to mitigate negative feelings that are stored in our bad memories. The recollection of an event will stay but without an emotional sting. In addition, we will explore how to learn actively from our past experiences. Again, the recollection of the event will be left, but more knowledge and experience would be extracted from that past episode.

COMMON PROBLEM:
Dwelling on the past

After something bad happens – let's say you made a mistake or someone treated you unfairly – it is normal for your mind to be drawn to this event and to think about it. It is a common, automatic and absolutely normal response. The point is that your brain simply tries to process what went wrong and figure out whether you are safe right now.

But if you find yourself thinking regularly about the same event, feeling unable to let it go, then it can be a sign that you have fallen into the trap of rumination. And that's not useful.

Simply put, rumination refers to thinking repetitively about something (usually a past event or a current stressor). Literally, the word 'rumination' means 'chewing the cud'. In this not very appetising process, an animal chews food, swallows, regurgitates and then chews it again (until it is digestible). Psychologically, our brains can act in a similar way. We may go over and over some information, reprocessing or reworking it, without completion.

Typically, a person tends to replay the same past event or stressor over and over again (e.g. lost opportunities, old injustices, memories of an ex, the times you misspoke, etc.). If you ever bombed a test, for example, you might play out the scene of getting the negative result over and over again.

In addition, in rumination it is also common to ask abstract questions about causes and consequences of the problem, such as: 'Why me?', 'Why do bad things happen to good people?', 'Why did she/he do that to me?'

Think about your own behaviour. If something upsets you, do you often fixate on it? Do you often replay the same incident over and over in your mind? Maybe you can't stop thinking about a painful break-up. Perhaps you mull over some unfair comments your boss made at work. Or you frequently recall some old mistake and obsess about what went wrong.

Why do we ruminate? Generally, it is connected to problem-solving. People ruminate because they expect to figure out what went wrong and why. By reviewing those episodes and different nuances connected to them, we are simply desperately seeking insight into how to fix the situation. For example, the logic is the following: *If I keep replaying the episode when my girlfriend dumped me, I will understand what is wrong with me.*

But the problem is that this kind of self-reflection tends to go awry. First of all, rumination offers very few valuable insights. When ruminating, people often tend to focus on how those events made them feel, rather than considering the situation critically and objectively. They don't gain any psychological distance from those events and get affected by painful emotions. Thereby, it is hard to find any valuable takeaway.

Second, there is no clear end point for when you can stop thinking about an issue. Basically, those who ruminate take this activity too far and for too long. They can ponder about the same issue for weeks, brooding over any tiny detail, imagining alternative scenarios, or thinking of what could have been if ... But the problem is that this thinking process can go on indefinitely.

Lastly, the worst thing is that rumination can take a toll on your overall wellbeing. If you refresh some past disappointment in your mind during the whole day, there is a good chance that you will feel bad during this day. However, if you fixate on a problem and regularly return to the past to rehearse old dissatisfactions, your emotional suffering increases dramatically. If nothing changes, this mental strain may ultimately result in emotional and physical breakdown.

Studies consistently find that rumination is strongly associated with numerous symptoms and mental disorders. The list includes stress, alcohol abuse, binge-eating, sleep disturbance, anxiety, depression and self-harm. Many people, for example, start using alcohol or food to take the edge off the pain and negativity that result from constant harping.

TRAINING GOAL:
Learn from the past

It seems as though, these days, thinking about the past is not very popular. If you google articles on the topic, the top results will be about how to forget the past, how to get over the past, or how to stop thinking about it.

It comes from an understandable place. On the one hand, books on mindfulness are more and more popular nowadays. The standard advice goes something like this: let go of the past, don't worry about the future, and live in the present. Basically, we're told that the present is essentially the only thing that matters. On the other hand, there is a common belief that the past is only for older people, who have already peaked and now spend time looking back on life. Or it is for those who are just afraid of change.

There is some truth to those views, of course. It is definitely not helpful to ruminate or dwell on past events for too long (see previous section, 'Dwelling on the past'). Neither is it good to miss the present moment.

Yet ignoring the past is not a good idea either. Do you remember Henry Molaison, the guy who suffered from amnesia (see Chapter 3)? He is the one who lived permanently in the present moment, being unable to recall what happened thirty seconds ago. It is unlikely that you would like to have the same kind of experience.

Let me highlight this point. Reminiscing and thinking about the past are healthy and normal processes. If you could not do that, then you would definitely be in trouble.

It is important to note that memories are not just the useless remnants of past events. Your memory is a powerful tool for teachings and guidance. By having memories, we know what happened, what worked well and what didn't. We can remember where we made a mistake and how to do things differently next time. Whether you realise it or not, you rely on your memories and experience all the time to judge how you should act in the present or in the future.

Suppose you're thinking about where to go on your holidays this year. In this process, you're actually quickly going over all the good and bad places you've ever been to. For example, you may recall one great time when you were chilling on a sunny beach in Portugal. After retrieving this episode, you may suddenly wish to repeat this experience again. In a split second, you may jump to the future and picture yourself sitting on a beach chair in front of the ocean with a piña colada in your hand.

In this context, one adaptive way of thinking about the past is called self-reflection (sometimes just referred to as reflection). Self-reflection may take different forms, but most commonly quality self-reflection involves two key components: non-judgemental attitude and active learning. Let's break it down.

Non-judgemental attitude	This means reviewing the episode as a non-judgemental observer. The aim is not to judge or criticise yourself or others but simply review how a certain event unfolded (see Practice #3: Zoom out).
Active learning	This refers to purposefully processing the episode with the goal to learn something and gain knowledge – which can then be used to solve a problem, make better choices next time or avoid the same situation in the future (see Practice #2: Reflect).

It is important to draw a clear line between self-reflection and rumination. Rumination is when you just replay past events over and over again, without purpose, or ask abstract questions that don't lead to anything useful. If you have a fight with your spouse, for example, you may just stew on what they said and recall all the times they did something wrong in your marriage.

By contrast, self-reflection is goal-oriented and productive. We are motivated by the desire to learn something from the experience, no matter how painful it was, and make improvements. Once we process the episode, and extract usable knowledge for future reference, we let it go.

For example, if you got into a fight with someone close to you and they let you know that something you do bothers them, you think back to those episodes, sort out whether that criticism is valid, and ask what you can do to fix it. Another example: after failing to deliver a project in time at work, you intentionally think through each step of the project development to figure out where you went wrong. Then you come up with a plan to avoid the same issue in the future, without beating yourself up for the mistake.

Why is this helpful? First of all, self-reflection is one of the best ways to grow and avoid future mistakes. I suppose this point speaks for itself. The goal of self-reflection, in essence, is to get knowledge. So, when you engage in this practice regularly, you, in fact, proactively work on your life experience and expand your knowledge system.

Second, self-reflection also allows you to reframe bad memories, transforming them into less disturbing or even supportive memories. This point may need more clarification.

Basically, for self-reflection to work, we need to come with the constructive attitude that we can learn something valuable even from the negative event. Of course, it does not deny the fact that something bad happened and that we felt bad, even terrible sometimes. We acknowledge what happened and how bad it felt. But we also recognise that each negative event can also be viewed as a learning opportunity. As a matter of fact, we often learn far greater lessons from negative events than from those days when everything was fine. That's because when we know how bad it feels, we are motivated not to repeat the same event again.

Now back to the memory. When you retrieve a bad memory and think that it was totally a negative experience, that memory remains bad. Nothing changes. The memory may become stronger and more distressing if you keep recalling it non-stop.

But if you retrieve the same bad memory and consider whether you can elicit anything valuable from it (such as a lesson, useful information or meaning), you actually reframe that event or change how you remember it.

What is the outcome? If you can identify at least one lesson, it is very likely that the original bad memory will become less painful. In some cases, you may even transform the original memory completely and turn it into a supportive one. For example, if you look back at a time when you failed and see how you gained wisdom from that situation, which helped you later on, that original bad memory might lose some of its sting.

Of course, it is easier said than done. But I will try to make it as simple as possible for you. 'Practice #1: Set aside time for review' will prepare you for the reflection time (the so-called review session). The next two practices will focus on reflection itself. 'Practice #2: Reflect' will spell out how to ask the right questions and identify lessons (the 'active learning' component of self-reflection). 'Practice #3: Zoom out' will explain how to review an episode as an external observer (the 'non-judgemental' component of self-reflection).

PRACTICE #1:
Set aside time for review

A review is when you look back at a certain period of time and examine what happened: what worked well, what didn't go so well, what can be changed. The general purpose of this exercise is to learn from a past experience to make changes and improve things in the future.

In fact, reviews originate from professional fields, in particular from medicine, management consulting and software development. They go by many names, such as post-mortems, retrospectives, performance reviews, project-success meetings, etc. Regardless of what you call them, they all have the same goal and follow a similar format. It is basically an 'improvement meeting' when teammates identify past mistakes or problems and find ways to improve and avoid the same issues in the future.

Ironically, most of us have annual performance reviews at work, create reports about what we've done for the business or for other people, but never take time to conduct a personal review to reflect on the course of our own life.

The easy way to motivate yourself to do this is to remember

that a personal review is the time when you extract knowledge, experience and wisdom from past events. Those who decide not to think about the past (if that is possible at all) simply miss out on realising their full potential. By contrast, those who harness their past experiences are those who are most prepared to make good decisions in the present and build a brighter future.

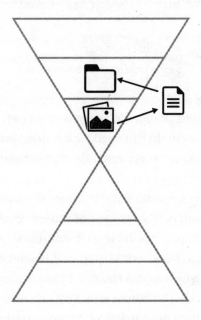

Extracting lessons from past events. Lessons can be viewed as files that are transferred and stored in our knowledge database (semantic memory).

To start with, we need to decide what kind of review we want to do. There are a few options, depending on how often you'd like to do this exercise:

- *Daily review* – Looking back on how your day was (e.g. fifteen minutes every evening before going to bed)

- *Weekly review* – Thinking back over the whole week (let's say, up to one hour every Sunday)

- *Monthly review* – Reflecting on the previous month (e.g. two hours on the last day of every month)

- *Annual review* – Reflecting on the last twelve months (e.g. designating the last weekend of December before the New Year).

So we can either do regular reviews every day with shorter sessions, or we can do this exercise less often but have longer reflection sessions. It all depends on your preferences and lifestyle.

I wouldn't suggest sticking just to annual reviews. Completing a personal review just once a year looks neither sufficient nor very productive. It will either take you too long to bring to mind everything that happened during the year, or you will just run the risk of skipping many important episodes that require your attention. Plus, you miss the chance to correct your behaviour more regularly and adjust the course in the middle of the year if needed.

On the flipside, doing reviews every day may not be the best idea either (unless, of course, you are already an experienced practitioner at this). It might be simply overwhelming to do the exercise every day if you are not used to it or have many other things to do during the day.

As a reasonable alternative, you may try a weekly or

monthly review and then see how it goes. At these check-points, the time periods will be long enough to think about and the episodes will still be fresh in your mind. On top of that, you can always perform a daily review occasionally, if the day was full of events or strong emotions and you don't want to postpone self-reflection till the end of the week or month.

The point of this exercise is to give yourself a chance to process your past adequately. Your brain needs some time to process the things that go on in your life, especially the trou-blesome past events. When you allocate some time 'to do the thinking', you can sort out things in a more productive manner.

The only thing that you need to do at this point is to pick a review type and incorporate it into your schedule. This will be beneficial for two reasons.

First of all, you won't forget to set aside time to do the review practice. In today's highly dynamic world, it is common to move at full speed. Many of us rush from one meeting to another, chase task after task, and constantly generate new plans. And the majority rarely take the time to pause and reflect on what they have already done and how well it went. For this reason, it is helpful to decide in advance to incorporate the review sessions into your schedule. No matter what happens in your life, you will always have fixed time slots to stop and ponder.

Second, you should also schedule endpoints to the rem-iniscing. Doing reviews is a great tool, for sure. But that's not a suggestion to start living in the past. Recollections can consume anyone, either when you engage in nostalgia over good old days, ruminate, or do a critical analysis. That's why we reserve a fixed period of time, let's say an hour, to do the thinking and try to stick to this time limit. Once sixty minutes is up, we stop the session.

Directions

1. *Schedule the review sessions* – Whatever strategy you choose, it is a good idea to schedule the time slots on your calendar in advance (e.g. twenty minutes on Sundays at 11 a.m.).

2. *Hold on* – If you notice yourself ruminating outside of that scheduled time, remind yourself that you will need to wait until your review session. *I will think about it later.* That's it. Just knowing that you can come back to a disturbing topic at a later time can help to quiet the chatter in your head.

3. *Write down the agenda* – If you feel too stressed, write down what bothers you in a notebook and tell yourself that you will address those issues during your review time.

4. *Conduct the session* – During that time period let yourself reflect on the past events in your life (how to do it effectively will be explained in Practice #2 and Practice #3). When your time is up, move on to something else.

PRACTICE #2:
Reflect

For the review itself, we can use a table with four columns. At the top of the columns, write 'Category', 'What went well?', 'What did not go so well'?, and 'What could be improved?'. Depending on your preferred method, you can do this in a notebook or on your laptop or tablet.

Once the table is ready, we can kick off the review session. Suppose it is a monthly review. In this case, you look back at your past month and reflect on different areas of your life, considering what went well, what was not so successful, and what can be improved. Below, I give more details on each section of the table.

Review table:

Category	What went well?	What did not go so well?	What could be improved?
Health/ fitness			
Job			
Family			
...			

1. Category
Categories refer to the different topics that you wish to review and work on. Personally, I tend to reflect on different

areas of my life rather than asking how life was in general. In the far-left column, I list either different areas of my life that I wish to work on, like 'family', 'work', 'health', or, if I want to be more specific, I add different roles that are present in my life, like being an 'author', 'partner', 'friend', 'brother', etc.

Here are some of the topics you might want to have in your table: career, finance, physical health, sport, family, friendship, romance and dating, fun and leisure, personal growth, home, spirituality. There is no right or wrong here, or 'one size fits all' – everyone chooses different categories. It all depends on what topic you deem important or relevant right now.

Having different categories is a great way to organise information. The table thus has small boxes for each specific topic. If you don't break down your life into different categories, it is very easy to be all over the place and lose track of those areas of life that require your attention.

2. What went well?
This is where you jot down all the things that went well during the last month. What were your wins? Was there something you were proud of? Were there any events that had a positive effect on you? This could be related to any of the categories you work on: career progression, health, hobbies, romantic life, etc. These could be big things, like getting a promotion or making a trip abroad. Or these could be really small, personal things, like cutting back on snacks or having a great time with friends on Saturday night. Did your boss compliment your work? Acknowledge that. Did you buy something pretty? Acknowledge that. Everyone

should have something positive to say, even if it is just: 'Hey, we are still alive!'

It is usually pretty easy to recall a handful of things that went well. If you are struggling, though, you may find it helpful to look through your calendar, look back over your to-do list, or check your social networks and glean some information from there.

It can be any number of things. Maybe you have just one thing that went right this month or maybe you have a dozen bullet points. Nothing is too small and nothing is too big for this exercise. Ideally, you should try to come up with at least one reason to give yourself a pat on the back.

By doing this exercise, we activate our positive memories. When we think about what went well, we are reminded that good things do happen in our life. You may bring some positive feelings into your present, conjure up evidence that you are loved and valued. With this in mind, it is much easier to maintain feelings of self-worth, to see the world in a more optimistic light, make right choices or bounce back from any setback.

3. What didn't go so well?

Next, you can get into the more difficult topic and think about what didn't go so well. This is where you specify your problems, disappointments and frustrations from the past month.

Here are some examples: making an error on a project, being late for a business meeting, having poor sleep during the last couple of weeks. You might realise that you have not spent enough time with your family lately or skipped workout sessions.

Let's face it, there is always room for improvement in every aspect of life. Even in a successful project, it is always possible to identify ways to make it better. That said, 'nothing negative to report' is also an answer.

Try to keep it neutral. Don't write how terrible you are at something. I don't want you to dwell on the negatives or beat yourself up with words. Instead, it is useful to pinpoint the root cause of the problem, whatever it might be. For example: 'I did not sleep well, probably because I started staying up until midnight watching TV.' These insights will feed into the next question about what can be improved.

This section is meant only to draw out areas of improvement. After all, where better to look for improvements than where things are not going so well? If we acknowledge that there is an issue, we can make some necessary changes and work towards correcting it the next month.

4. What could be improved?

The previous column lists our observations of the things that did not go so well, which invites the question: 'How could we improve?'

The goal of the final column is to identify what actions need to be taken to improve in the future. What can we do to make sure we don't run into the same situation again? What can we do to prevent the problem from recurring? What steps do we need to take to mitigate the issue?

This can be something small. It is enough to pick one or two concrete actions. You can write down a simple phrase for anything related to your career, home, romance, finance, or any other area in need of improvement. For example, it could be: 'Taking notes prior to scheduling a call', 'Joining a yoga class', 'Finishing a book I'm reading'. It could be something as simple as: 'Create a calendar reminder to . . .'

The more measurable you can make these actions, the better. For example, instead of saying that you should go to bed earlier to have a better sleep, you can establish the exact time when you intend to go to bed every day, let's say, at 11 p.m.

Lastly, it is important to track your progress. Revisit your notes from the previous month before completing the next review. If you follow your improvement plan, you will see the improvements next month. If you see the same issues continuing to find their way into the 'What didn't go so well' column for two months in a row, it may indicate that you did not carry out the plan or that it was not effective enough.

Example

Category	What went well?	What did not go so well?	What could be improved?
Health/ fitness	Joined a gym after a long break.	Started skipping stretching exercises in the evening.	Set a reminder in my calendar to do stretching twice a week.

Category	What went well?	What did not go so well?	What could be improved?
Job	Had less workload during the last month, had more time for self-education.	Ignored one of the tasks, which caused problems at work.	Pay attention to all tasks that have 'priority 1'.

PRACTICE #3:
Zoom out

Ready for a thought experiment? Take a moment and revisit one of your memories. It can be any memory at all – a recent activity or something from the distant past. For example, you may want to recount what you did this morning step by step. As you travel through that memory, think of how you see yourself in that moment. Do you see the events through your own eyes, as you experienced the situation originally? Or do you see yourself from the outside, as a bystander would?

People have a unique ability to reflect on their experience from different perspectives. There are two perspectives from which we can view a memory: a first-person perspective and a third-person perspective.

First-person perspective (also known as a field or self-immersed perspective) is when you view or recall events through your own eyes, as you experienced the situation the first time. Basically, it is the usual or default way to recall events. When we remember events in this way, it may feel as if we are reliving and re-experiencing the situation over again.

Third-person perspective (also known as an observer or self-distanced perspective) is when you recall events not from the original point of view but from the outside, as an observer would. When you engage in this third-person recall, it looks like you are watching yourself in a movie.

Let's say, for example, Leo is recalling the moment when he received a job offer. From the first-person perspective, Leo remembers the moment just as he experienced it originally. He hears his phone ringing on a table, he sees his right hand reaching out to pick it up, he recognises the recruiter's voice, and he re-experiences the feeling of surprise and joy. Now let's switch to the third-person view. If Leo were to take the third-person perspective, he would remember this moment as if he were another person who were in that room that day. He would see how a young man (named Leo) hears a phone ringing, walks across the room, picks a up the phone and says hello. He would then notice that young man smile.

Now let's get back to bad memories. When we replay negative events, we generally tend to take a first-person perspective, seeing the events through our own eyes. And that's a trap. When we take a first-person perspective, we immerse ourselves in the past situation again. We replay the details of that event and re-experience what we felt at that time. Simply put, we relive the event from the emotional point of view. Even worse, we often get caught up in all of the emotionally arousing details of that event and start to ruminate about what happened, why it was wrong, how it made us feel, which only intensifies negative feelings.

However, as we reflect on a difficult episode from the past, we can also adopt the third-person perspective and view the episode from the vantage point of a bystander. It is like taking a look at your own struggles as if you were looking at them through the eyes of another person – a person who is not directly involved in the episode.

Let's do an experiment. Think of some memory that causes *moderate* distress to you – e.g. a failure at work, a conflict with a friend, being late for an important appointment, etc. As you view the disturbing memory, shift your perspective from the first person to the third person. Zoom out from the recollection until you can see yourself within the scene. Zoom out further so that you can see the whole scene: its participants and events. Then play it out and watch the events unfold as if you were a distant onlooker.

Feels different? This simple manipulation is designed to help create some psychological distance between you and the memory. By doing the exercise, you basically step out of your own direct experiences, which helps to reduce the emotional charge of the memory to some extent. The emotion is still felt, but it does not have a sting any more.

But I want to highlight that this exercise is not designed to work with PTSD, flashbacks or any other highly traumatic issue. If you do struggle with the effects of a traumatic experience, it is a good idea to look for a psychotherapist who is able to work with such issues.

Visual summary

Common problem:
Dwelling on the past

Training goal:
Learn from the past

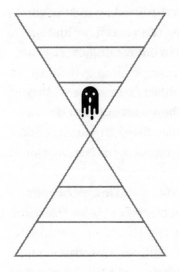

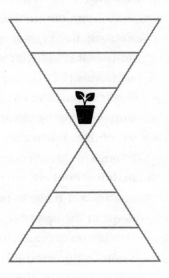

──────── **Chapter summary** ────────

- Along with the event itself, our brain can also record the emotions experienced during this event. Emotions tend to make memories sharp and vivid. If the event is emotionally significant, it is much easier to remember. The more significant the event is, the more likely you are to commit it to memory.

- If the emotion is strong and painful, it then creates a strong and painful memory that can be involuntarily and easily triggered by different clues in your environment.

- It often feels that bad memories have a life of their own. All these 'spirits' can be a source of great distress in our life. When they strike, they can drag us back to negative experiences, weigh us down and increase negative thoughts.

- Rumination refers to repetitive thinking about some event in the past or a current stressor. Overthinking results in emotional distress.

- Self-reflection refers to thinking about a past event with a non-judgemental attitude and with the goal of learning something valuable (even from the negative experience).

- Conduct personal monthly reviews to reflect on different areas of your life. Ask yourself what lesson you can learn from it and how you could do better in the future.

- Adopt a third-person perspective to review painful memories. Visualise yourself as a stranger who happened to pass by and who can observe the events unfolding from afar.

Part Two

Visual summary

Common problems:
Zoning out, negative
self-talk, dwelling
on the past

Training goals: Develop
mindfulness, think
realistically, learn
from the past

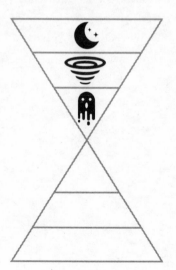

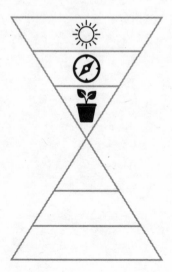

	Common problem	Training goal	Practice
1. Reason	Zoning out	Develop mindfulness	1) Come back 2) Five senses 3) Meditate
2. Belief	Negative self-talk	Think realistically	1) Monitor 2) Thought Record 3) Challenge
3. Memories	Dwelling on the past	Learn from the past	1) Set aside time 2) Reflect 3) Zoom out

You can also do the aforementioned exercises digitally with the help of the Brightway journaling app. You can download the app free at www.brightway.app, from the App Store or from Google Play. There is also a 'How to Use the App' page at the end of this book for more information.

Part Three

The Bottom Pyramid

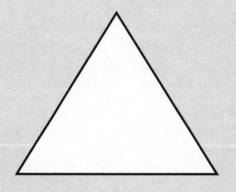

8

Master of Emotions

Many people are confused by their emotions. Why are we made to feel so much? Why do our feelings seem so irrational sometimes? What purpose do our emotions serve?

The most common view is that emotions play an important evolutionary role in survival. All emotions – whether negative or positive – exist for a reason. Although anger, fear, guilt or others from this list are not the ones we love most, all of them serve an important purpose. The reality is that each emotion proved to be useful at some point in our evolution to help us cope with different situations. Simply put, emotions draw us to things that feel good and away from things that feel bad. For example, disgust stops you from being poisoned, fear pushes you to avoid danger, joy signals that you are safe, while love prompts you to mate and look after offspring.

Relatedly, the emotion system* is designed to induce a quick response to various situations. When our ancestors

---

* The limbic system and the amygdala – the part of the brain that is heavily implicated in emotion.

lived in the wild, they needed to react quickly when faced with danger. Imagine you meet a tiger. There is no time to think. You need to act fast or be eaten. For this reason, emotions can take over and grab the wheel that steers our behaviour. They kick off an immediate response and spur our body to take action accordingly. In a split second, adrenaline is released into the bloodstream, the heart begins to race and the muscles tighten. As a result, your body is prepared either to run away or fight for your life.

The take-home message is: emotions are useful signals. They are there to tell you what is helpful and what is dangerous. For example, if you are threatened in some way, fear alarms you that you may need to run and protect yourself. Without fear, you would not consider any risks, and thus you would put your life in danger all the time.

If you ignore your emotions, you simply disconnect from important messages that your brain is sending you. But when you listen to your emotions, you learn valuable information about what is going on. You get insight into what is going inside you. You get more knowledge of what you need, what is troubling you, how you are affected by your environment as well as by your own thoughts and actions. Knowing this can help you strengthen the connection with yourself, make more informed choices, and ultimately feel good.

COMMON PROBLEM:
Emotional overwhelm

Some people don't want to have negative feelings at all. Sometimes you wish that you could always be happy, don't you? I must remind you, however, that having negative feelings is not a problem. No emotion is 'wrong'. All feelings – whether positive or negative – are meant to be felt.

However, if you experience an emotional overwhelm, that can be a problem. Emotional overwhelm is a state of being under *intense* emotions. You can tell that you are in this state when feelings are so strong that you find it hard to cope with them.

Emotional overwhelm entails more than feeling bad or stressed out. By definition, being overwhelmed means being flooded or overcome by something. When it comes to emotional overwhelm, it means that you are completely submerged by rough and unruly emotions. Imagine a 20ft wave crashing down on you. It is a terrifying experience. The moment when the wave engulfs you, you feel trapped, helpless, not knowing which way is up and unable to swim away.

Typically, we are most likely to get overwhelmed by negative feelings, such as fear, anger, guilt or shame. You are probably familiar with the phrase 'overwhelmed with grief', which may happen when a person loses a loved one. However, it is also possible to be overwhelmed by positive emotions, such as joy, for example. Feeling ecstatic or euphoric are common examples.

It does not really matter whether we talk about negative or positive emotions. What matters is that feelings build up to a critical point, reaching a threshold at which it becomes difficult to manage them.

Have you ever felt like your emotions were completely out

of control? For example, have you ever lost your temper and said something that you later regretted? Or maybe you were feeling numb in response to a series of life problems. Maybe you missed some important opportunities because of fear. Perhaps you went down the spiral to sadness, even feeling depressed. If so, you are not alone.

How one person experiences emotional overwhelm can look very different to how another person goes through this state. It can show up differently depending on the emotion and the person. But here are some common signs that you are feeling overwhelmed:

- Facing increased negative emotions (e.g. anxiety, irritability, guilt, sadness)
- Overreacting to seemingly insignificant situations (e.g. snapping at people, crying out or getting angry without an obvious reason)
- Feeling physically unwell (e.g. raised blood pressure, shortness of breath, sweating, headache, weakened immune system, insomnia, fatigue)
- Struggling to get things done.

What causes emotional overwhelm? If a person encounters a life stressor and feels that it is too big to deal with, they become overwhelmed. Often, emotional overwhelm is caused by a single significant stressor, such as surviving a car accident or losing a loved one. Alternatively, it can stem from a series of challenges or adversities that occur simultaneously or in succession, such as stress at work and problems in relationships. In such cases, it can be difficult for a person to identify the exact causes of their unwieldy emotions.

It should be noted here that what causes emotional overwhelm differs from person to person. The thing is what one person finds stressful may not be a big deal or may feel manageable for another person. Yet here are some common triggers of emotional overwhelm:

- Relationship issues (e.g. fighting, divorce proceedings)
- Stressful time at work (e.g. working long hours)
- Financial insecurity or poverty
- Poor nutrition
- Insomnia
- Physical or mental illness
- Traumatic personal experience (e.g. car accident, abuse)
- Death of a loved one
- Being a caregiver
- Raising children.

Needless to say, emotional overwhelm can affect a person in some pretty damaging ways. When you are feeling overwhelmed, you will find it hard to stay positive and to make sound decisions, which naturally will affect your personal and professional life. Moreover, if left unchecked, emotional overwhelm can wreak havoc on almost all your body's processes and put your physical and mental health at serious risk.

TRAINING GOAL:
Improve emotional regulation

At some point in life, we all struggle to cope with our emotions. If negative emotions spin out of control, we can go astray, fly off the handle and then regret things said or done in the heat of the moment. Again, it is not that positive emotions are good, and negative emotions are bad. Positive emotions – like too much excitement, for example – can cause a lot of trouble in the wrong context. When we have an over-optimistic outlook, for example, we can get too confident with ourselves, miscalculate risks and make unsound decisions.

Our goal is not to cultivate only positive emotions and force negative emotions out of our head. This strategy will backfire on you. A better way to go is to develop emotional self-regulation.

Emotional regulation (or emotional self-regulation) is a term generally used to describe a person's ability to recognise and manage their emotions in helpful ways. A person with strong emotional regulation can manage which emotions they have, how intense they are, when they have them, and how they express them.

To be more exact, good emotional regulation involves monitoring, enhancing, tempering, or modifying your emotions according to the demands of a situation or your goals. 'Down-regulation', for example, refers to reducing the intensity of your emotions. An anxious person, for instance, can down-regulate her anxiety by doing breathing exercises. An angry person may decide to distract herself by going for a run. 'Up-regulation', on the other hand, means increasing the intensity of your emotions on purpose. For example, if your team won the championship, to boost your happiness, you may decide to go and celebrate with other fans.

Note that emotional regulation does not mean that you never have negative emotions. It means that you know how to cope with your negative emotions in a helpful way. To put it simply, you have the tools to be able to calm down and you understand when and how to express your negative emotions constructively.

Suppose your boss lashes out at you for a mistake you made at work. How would you react? Would you shout back at him during a business meeting? Would you decide to quit the job? Or would you handle your frustration without an outburst or bottling up your anger? If the latter, congratulations, you have a good level of emotional self-regulation.

But note that there are degrees of emotional regulation. Some people may be naturally more skilful, or they may be better trained, than others. Picture the scene: your boss shouts at you in the morning. Later that day, someone in the street spills coffee on your new shirt. On your way home, you are cut up in traffic. And when back home, your spouse yells at you for doing something wrong. So how would you respond to all those situations?

Suppose you manage to keep your nerves under control in each of those situations, without suppressing your anger. In this case, you are a Jedi master and you can have your own apprentices.

However, in the above example, a person may be able to regulate his or her emotions at work and fail to do so in the other situations. You may be able to hold back your anger at work but have an outburst while driving. Or you may remain calm in traffic but get into a fight with your spouse at home.

Without doubt, it is worth developing our emotional regulation skills. Good emotional regulation skills provide numerous immediate and long-term benefits, such as increased psychological wellbeing, increased physical health, being able to cope with life stressors, keeping an emotional balance, performing better and having more peaceful relationships.

Let's assume you have great difficulty keeping your temper. Don't worry. Emotional regulation is not a skill we are born with. It is something we learn as we grow up. Take children as an example. When faced with discomfort, children lose their temper like crazy. They throw tantrums, burst out crying and exhibit a complete lack of self-control. The fact is that children are at the very early stage of their emotional self-regulation. But they can improve on it. If parents or caregivers explain to children how to cope with their emotions, they can gradually learn how to mitigate their feelings and respond to situations that may upset them. So, as a grown-up, you probably no longer throw a tantrum in the street when you are tired or don't get an ice cream.

If you find it hard to manage your emotions, it may be that you've never been taught how to do that. But the good news is that emotional regulation is a skill. It can be practised and improved to some degree at any stage of life. Here are some techniques that you can try to integrate into your daily routine.

PRACTICE #1:
Label

Have you ever said: 'I am upset', 'I'm scared', or 'I'm angry' out loud? If yes, well done! In reality, lots of people find it hard to name what they are feeling, not to mention face their negative emotions head-on. Instead, many try to sweep their negative feelings under the carpet. That's understandable – nobody wants to feel bad. However, if we want to develop our emotional self-regulation skills, it is advisable to do quite the opposite. We need to learn to label or to name negative emotions as they arise. This is the most basic technique that we can have in our toolkit.

Whenever you are out of sorts, ask yourself some screening questions. What am I feeling right now? Am I sad? Do I feel disappointed? Am I angry? After that, put a name to the feeling that is active at that moment. For example, you can say simply 'Anger', or 'I feel angry', or 'I feel sad'.

As a psychologist, I frequently ask people: 'What do you feel?' or 'How did that make you feel?' This is probably the most common question psychotherapists ask their clients. And it is also often the most annoying one for the majority.

What makes this question annoying is that naming emotions is not as easy as it may sound. Despite the huge role that emotions play in our life, most of us do not think very often about how we feel ourselves. That's why many people have great trouble in distinguishing between different emotional states. They simply do not have the skill to do that.

When asked about feelings, I commonly hear people

respond simply: 'I don't know.' Alternatively, some folk come up with very generic descriptions like 'great', 'fine', 'okay', 'terrible', or 'not bad', without specifying any actual emotion. I know a few individuals who use only two words to describe the whole palette of their emotional life. They feel either 'good' or 'bad'.

I wonder whether you track how you feel during the day? Let's do a quick experiment. How are you feeling right now? Hold on for a second. Can you name the dominant emotion? Maybe there are a few emotions at play right now? Okay, let's dig a bit deeper. How did you feel two hours ago? Don't rush with an answer. All right, moving on. Think of how you felt yesterday? Take note that you probably had lots of different feelings during the day. But can you name at least one?

Again, naming emotions is not an easy task. There is still a debate among researchers as to how many basic emotions people actually have. The famed American psychologist Paul Ekman identified six universal emotions – joy, anger, sadness, disgust, fear and surprise. Yet, according to a study by researchers at the University of California, Berkeley, there are actually twenty-seven distinct emotions.

Either way, it is a bit tricky to identify all the gradients and the boundaries between different emotions. That's why researchers still struggle to map the whole spectrum of our emotional life.

While the debate continues, researchers tend to agree that there are at least five basic emotions: joy, anger, disgust, sadness and fear. This is where you can start.

But you can also extend your emotional awareness with some understanding of other emotional states. As a rule of thumb, these are considered as some of the most common emotional states:

Joy	Sympathy	Fear	Sadness	Anger
Excitement	Craving	Surprise	Pain	Irritability
Admiration	Love	Horror	Grief	Resentment
Amusement	Boredom	Anxiety	Guilt	Disgust
Awe	Calmness	Shock	Regret	Contempt
Happiness	Loneliness	Panic	Shame	Fury
			Embarrassment	Jealousy
				Envy
				Pride

Are you familiar with all of those emotions? Do you know the difference, for example, between feeling embarrassed and feeling ashamed? How about jealousy and envy? When was the last time you felt amused? Are there any emotions that you think you do not experience at all or feel very rarely? I understand that all these questions can be annoying and frustrating. Believe me, I do. But if you can think about them, you may become a little bit more informed about your emotional life.

It is also worth noting that some people believe that they can feel only one thing at a time. But keep in mind that it is possible to feel a mix of emotions at the same time. While awaiting the results of a job interview, for example, you can be both anxious, impatient and excited.

Moreover, it is possible to feel both positive and negative emotions at the same time. Thinking of people we have lost, for instance, we can feel both grief and sadness because of the loss, and gratitude for the fact that they were once in our life.

What's the point of this exercise? First and foremost, this exercise is designed to reduce the intensity of your feelings. The thing is that when you name what you feel, you actually soothe that emotion – be it positive or negative.

It is all down to how our brain functions. When a person experiences a strong emotion, the emotional brain regions are activated and run the show (the limbic system). But when you label what you're feeling, you activate your rational brain regions (the prefrontal cortex), which reduce the arousal of the emotional brain regions. The prefrontal cortex helps you with thinking, finding solutions and problem-solving. So when you say 'I am feeling angry' or just 'Anger', for example, the prefrontal cortex gets to work and you turn the emotion into an object of scrutiny.

In addition, by doing this exercise you also create a psychological distance between you and the emotion. When you name an emotion, this reminds you that you are not your feelings. Yes, you may be angry now, but this feeling is temporary. On the one hand, you listen to what you're feeling. But on the other hand, you step back and avoid getting caught up in the emotional storm.

If you are not used to paying attention to your emotions and this exercise makes you uncomfortable, don't worry. It is just a skill, so you can get better with practice.

PRACTICE #2:
Breath

Breath is one of the most overlooked and yet one of the most powerful tools in a self-care practitioner's toolkit. It can ease stress, reduce anger, make you feel less anxious or boost energy levels.

Let's start with the basics. What we know from studies is that emotions and breath are closely connected. For one thing, emotions elicit different breathing patterns – for example, holding our breath in fear; sighing in relief. You may also notice that in moments of stress, your breathing becomes fast, irregular and shallow. By contrast, in calmer times – when you feel relaxed – your breath becomes slower, longer and deeper.

The important fact is that the relationship between emotions and breathing is not just one-way. Just as emotions can lead to different breathing patterns, our breathing can make us feel different things. Why is that important for us? Basically, we can use breath to change how we feel.

You probably don't think much about your breath, do you? Breathing is one of the few bodily processes that can be either automatic or consciously controlled. Normally, breathing is an automatic process that occurs without thinking about it. It is always there, even when you sleep. Yet we can also consciously control our breath – making it longer or shorter, holding it, etc. It is called controlled breathing.

There are lots of controlled breathing techniques, and the right one for you will depend on your goals. Here, we will learn the so-called diaphragmatic breathing (also known as deep breathing). This is one of the most basic and effective techniques to control stress levels.

Let me first explain what diaphragmatic breathing is. There are two types of breathing patterns: chest breathing and diaphragmatic breathing. Chest breathing is characterised by engaging upper chest muscles and involves shallow and rapid breaths. This type of breathing leads to minimal oxygen intake, shortening breath, and a feeling of alertness. It typically occurs when a person works out or faces an emergency situation. But many people get into the habit of breathing through their chest most of the time. That's not good, as shallow breathing can keep the body in a state of stress.

Diaphragmatic breathing (also known as belly or abdominal breathing) is a type of breathing that engages your diaphragm and involves taking deep breaths in. The diaphragm is a muscle at the bottom of your ribcage which helps you to breathe. The diaphragm does most of the work during the inhalation part. As you breathe in, the diaphragm contracts and moves downward, causing your belly to rise. This creates extra space in your chest cavity, allowing the lungs to expand and fill with air. Naturally, this helps to get enough air into your lungs. This type of breathing happens most commonly when you are asleep or relaxed. This is also the way babies and children naturally breathe.

Let's get back to stress management. The simplest way to relax is to take diaphragmatic breaths. Deep breaths will lower blood pressure, slow heart rate, relax muscles and calm the nervous system. As a result, you will feel calmer and more relaxed.

A simple way to check whether you are deep breathing is to use your hands. Place your right hand on your stomach and your left hand on your chest. As you breathe, notice which hand is moving. Most of the movement should happen at the bottom. As you inhale, you should feel the hand on your stomach move outwards. When you exhale, your bottom hand will move inwards. The hand on your chest should remain still or move only slightly.

The beauty of this exercise is that you can do it any time and anywhere. Breathing is something that is always with us throughout the day. You can thus do a breathing exercise at any point of the day when you feel uptight – e.g. while at work, sitting in traffic, when having to go into an interview, or after getting into an argument with a partner. In moments like these, all we have to do is take deep and slow breaths for a few minutes.

Directions

1. *Get ready* – Sit or lie down in a comfortable position. If you are sitting down, make sure that you keep your back straight. Allow your belly to relax. Allow your shoulders to relax – let them drop. You may find it helpful to close your eyes, though it is not necessary (when your eyes are closed, it can be easier to stay focused on your breathing mechanics and you won't be distracted by external stimuli).

2. *Focus on your breath* – Take a few breaths as you would usually do. Don't try to change anything at this point. Just become aware of your breathing pattern – notice whether your breathing is

rapid or slow, and whether there are any pauses between the inhalation and exhalation.

3. *Take some deep breaths* – Now, start breathing from your belly. Take a slow deep breath through your nose, allowing your belly to expand as far as it is comfortable. Let the air coming through your nostrils go deep down into your lower belly. Make sure that you keep your belly relaxed, without forcing it or clenching your muscles.

4. *Breathe out* – Then slowly exhale through your mouth.

5. *Add counting* – It can be helpful to count while you are breathing. For example, take a deep breath while slowly counting from one to five in your head. Then breathe out slowly to the count of five. And then again: inhale slowly to the count of five. And exhale, counting slowly to five. With practice, it will become easier to lengthen your breaths. Once you feel comfortable with breaths that last five counts, you can work up to counts of seven or more.

6. *Go on* – Keep taking deep breaths until you feel relaxed. Let your abdomen expand and contract with each breath. You might want to set a time

limit of three to ten minutes, or longer if needed. With practice, you will get an idea of how much time you need to relieve stress and reap other benefits.

PRACTICE #3:
Investigate

It is normal to experience ups and downs from time to time. You may even feel low a few times across the day. It is a part of being human. The good news is that most negative emotions pass through relatively quickly, making space for other emotions. Yet sometimes negative emotions persist. They don't seem to go away or they keep coming back. You manage to shake them off for a moment, using the deep breathing exercise, for example, but before long you start feeling bad again.

In this case, it may indicate that there is some hidden trigger at play that brings up your negative feelings. And the problem is that we are often oblivious to those triggers. Have you ever felt low, irritated, anxious or plain bad without knowing exactly why? You might be depressed and not know why. You might be worked up and not understand where it comes from. You may start crying all of a sudden, for no apparent reason.

Not knowing what causes you to feel so bad is a problem. Because you don't know where it comes from, you don't understand what may help, what to do to start feeling better.

Thus many people may spend days, weeks or months – if not longer – in the dark about what is going on with them emotionally.

It is important to remember that the emotions system is sort of our inner alarm system. And our emotions are the alerts. Negative emotions don't just arrive out of the blue. The main job of negative emotions is to get you to see a problem, so that you can cope with a situation. If the alarm goes off regularly, it simply means that something is going wrong. And your job as the owner of the house is to work out what is going on, why the system is being triggered, and then make the necessary changes.

The long story short: if you repeatedly experience a certain negative emotion, like anger, shame, guilt, anxiety or sadness, that's an indicator to take some time and investigate what's getting you down. To put it differently, we should do some research and pinpoint the causes of those lingering feelings. That is the only way to turn those feelings around.

There are many factors that determine how we feel. And sometimes it is difficult to place what these are. Yet, I would recommend taking a look at your thoughts first, as they are one of the main things that affects how we feel.

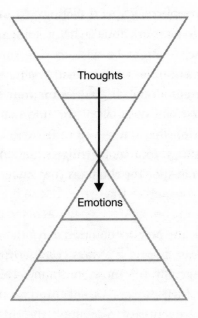

Consider what kind of thoughts are going through your mind. If you pause for a bit of self-reflection and check, you may catch a thought that provokes the emotional turmoil. Maybe you expected your spouse to help you more with your children, but she or he did not. Or you assume that you should blame yourself for things that have gone wrong. Or perhaps you assume that the worst possible scenario is going to happen.

If you do catch a disturbing thought, you already know how to deal with such intruders (see Chapter 6). It will involve analysing whether the thought is accurate, considering the evidence for and against the thought, disputing it and replacing it with a more balanced and realistic thought.

Suppose, after this quick screening, you still can't figure

out why you have some strong feelings. Don't be discouraged. To get to the root of our feelings is not always easy.

In this case, it might be wise to seek support from a professional mental health specialist. You never have to go through your emotional difficulties on your own. A good psychotherapist will piece all of the information together and will unravel what causes you to feel this way. You will get to understand your main triggers, and then you can become better at spotting them on your own.

Example

Whether you are new to emotional regulation or you're already a master, I suggest always considering Practice #1: Label. It is arguably the most common technique in the arsenal of most self-care practitioners and psychotherapists. Labelling is relatively easy to do. But at the same time, it can take a lot of the sting out of negative emotions. And it can give you important information to make changes in your behaviour or life overall.

To illustrate: in one study, researchers explored eighty-eight people with a fear of spiders. The experiment started by asking the participants to get as close as possible to a large, live tarantula in an open container and eventually touch the spider if they could. Then the participants sat in front of another tarantula and described their experience.

The first group was instructed to label what they were feeling – saying, for instance: 'I am scared and even terrified by this huge and ugly spider.' The second group tried to think differently about the spider and make their experience less threatening – saying, for example: 'I should not be afraid. That spider can't hurt me.' The third group said some irrelevant things, and the fourth did not say anything at all.

A week later the researchers repeated the procedure and asked the participants to approach the spider again and touch it if possible. It was found that the group that labelled their emotions did far better than the other groups. They walked closer to the spider and were much less distressed.

These results suggest that talking about our feelings could have a very powerful effect. At the very least, when people name their fears, talk about them – even if it is a terror of spiders – it can reduce their anxiety.

Visual summary

Common problem:
Emotional overwhelm

Training goal:
Emotional regulation

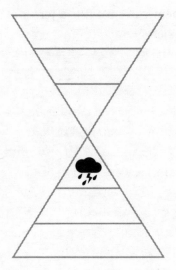

──────── Chapter summary ────────

- Rather than denying or suppressing negative emotions, be open and curious about your emotional landscape.

- If you are in a situation that evokes strong emotions, take a mental note of the range of emotions that you are experiencing. Use a single word or phrase to name what you feel. For example: 'Anger', 'Sadness' or 'I feel angry, sad'.

- One of the simplest techniques to reduce stress is controlled breathing. Controlled breathing is the voluntary regulation of breath – e.g. making it slower, longer, etc.

- You can start with diaphragmatic, or deep, breathing – consciously taking deep, slow breaths, actively using your diaphragm. Deep breathing encourages the body to relax and the mind to calm down.

- You can sneak a deep breathing exercise into your schedule, let's say, when you wake up, standing at a bus stop, sitting at your desk, or going to bed.

- If negative feelings keep coming back, it makes sense to stop and investigate the causes of those feelings. A good place to start is to check your thoughts. Are there any automatic thoughts that disturb you and affect how you feel?

9

Master of Words

We are all surrounded by stories. We watch them in movies, we read them in books, and learn about them from the news. What we don't always realise is that we constantly create our own stories.

You may not be aware of this, but people mostly communicate in a narrative form. Pay attention to how people are talking on the phone, in business meetings, or sitting at the bar. What you will quickly notice is that they tend to communicate through storytelling.

When someone asks you: 'Hey, how are you doing?', you may respond with just a few words, 'Good thanks! You?' and leave it at that. Of course, this is not a story. But if you decide to say more than one sentence, you are about to create a short narrative.

Talking to a friend, for example, it is common to share an anecdote of how you feel or what happened lately. For example, you may respond: 'Pretty good thanks! Guess what? They finally called and invited me for a job interview! I've been wondering what kind of questions they might ask me ...' Or it could be: 'You know, there is a new jazz club down the street. Jill booked a table last week, and it was absolutely amazing. The food, the music ...'

In short, a story is an easy way to organise and pass on our experience; to recount what happened, how we feel about it, and what we think about it. It is a tool to put random pieces of information together, to find meaning, and to understand life events as something coherent and as a whole.

Because of this, storytelling has been an integral part of human history since ancient times. It looks like the first story appeared once our species evolved the ability to use language to communicate. Researchers believe that the oldest story ever told is around 44,000 years old. It is a cave painting discovered by archaeologists on the Indonesian island of Sulawesi, which depicts a story of people hunting wild animals.

And of course, we remain prolific storytellers nowadays. As we go about our daily life, we create and tell loads of stories. We tell stories about our relationships, about our career, about politics, sex, movies, family, sports and wedding days. It may be a story of how your sports team won a match last week, or how you plan to spend your next weekend, or why you did not ask your crush to go out with you, or why you like Italian food, and so on.

There is an age-old saying that everyone has a book inside them. Given the number of stories we tell, I would say that each person is like a walking library. Returning home after work, we share these stories with our loved ones. Other days we recount them to our colleagues or post them on our social networks (our modern cave walls).

In turn, when we meet people and want to understand them better, we ask them to share their stories with us. Think of your last date. Or recall your last job interview. It is basically an exchange of stories between two people. 'Tell me a little bit about yourself!' And you jump to tell a prepared narrative of what you do, where you studied, why you like dogs more than cats, what you are looking for in relationships, or why you are the best candidate for the job.

Funnily enough, right now, I am telling you a story about what a story is. I hope this makes sense. In this book overall, however, I am telling a story of how to manage your mind and work on your mental health. It is an example of a long story, which consists of many sub-stories. It requires the whole book to tell and many years of research to create, packing in my life experiences, a myriad of thoughts, insights, memories and even feelings.

And soon you will do the same thing. When you are done reading this chapter, you will probably create your own story about it, maybe about this section as well, and then about the whole book. It might be a positive story if you found something interesting or useful, or it might be a critical story if you disliked the material. In addition, you may keep this story to yourself or decide to share it in a conversation with a friend or even write a review about it to share with the public.

I hope you get the general idea. Let's now talk a bit about technicalities. One important question is: 'How do we create stories?' Basically, there are two important stages.

At first, we start to construct our stories silently in our belief system, when we interpret different situations and try to take some meaning from what happened. Many people don't even notice this stage, as this process happens subconsciously. If you have ever caught yourself absorbed in contemplation or muttering something to yourself, let's say after an argument with your partner or just going about your business, that's it.

In the second stage, we move on to verbalise our stories in daily conversations. That is when it is very easy to spot our stories, as we can hear what we are actually telling or sharing with other people. Ultimately, if we keep verbalising a particular story for some time, we can form a verbal habit to do so. It means that we can begin to tell a certain story on autopilot, without thinking too much.

Of course, as soon as we form a verbal habit, we tend to repeat or replay a particular story in daily life. Whether you realise it or not, you often tell the same stories for months and even years. Think of your friends or family. I bet you've noticed your parents or friends retelling the same 'good' or 'bad' stories for years – be it funny incidents from their school years, how they managed to win some big tournament, what they did on holiday many years ago, or how they met the love of their life, or someone broke their heart, or explanations of why they are not married.

In conclusion, I must say that stories are more than just words. A growing body of research suggests that stories have a great impact on our life. How you tell your stories affects not only your listeners and whether they find you interesting or not. It turns out that the way you tell your stories can affect your mental wellbeing.

Stories about our own lives have a particular power. To illustrate this quickly, if you weave a self-story, for example, of being unfortunate or awkward on dates, it naturally makes it very hard for you to feel confident the next time you go out with anyone. By contrast, if you tell a story about how competent or playful you are while interacting with new people, you'd achieve the opposite effect, feeling more optimistic and determined.

How come? The thing is that our language does not exist in a vacuum from the rest of the mind. What you regularly say can easily affect how you feel, reinforce your beliefs about yourself, influence decisions you take and ultimately shape what kind of person you become.

COMMON PROBLEM:
Contamination stories

The ending is the crucial part of any story – a bad ending could easily ruin a great tale. That's something any author can tell you. After *A Farewell to Arms* was published, Ernest Hemingway revealed that he rewrote the ending thirty-nine times. Why? Because he was very concerned with 'getting the words right'.

It seems Hemingway intuitively understood something very important: since the ending is the last part of the story to reveal itself, it is what the readers will particularly remember when they think back to it. However, what Hemingway supposedly did not know was that it was equally important to think about how to create good endings in our personal stories, in the stories about our own life.

A type of story that contains bad endings, and which was well-researched by psychologists, is known as a 'contamination story'. Contamination stories start off good but turn bad at the end. Even if there is some good event at the beginning of a story, it then becomes destroyed, spoiled or erased (contaminated) by the negative events that follow.

To be fair, it is very easy to end a story badly when we face a failure or a dramatic loss. Examples are countless: missing an important goal, being laid off, going through a bad break-up, divorce, death, terminal illness, etc.

Here are a few examples of contamination stories to give you a sense of what I am talking about:

- 'When I was seventeen years old, I was fascinated by politics and economics [good beginning] ... But I chose the wrong university to study the subject and as a result wasted the next four years of my life. Now every time I look at my CV, I think that I made a huge mistake. I wish I had been smarter and chosen a better place to study [contamination].'

- 'We had a happy family ... We raised children together ... hoping to grow old together [good beginning] ... But we split up ... I'm now a single mother, and my life is a mess [contamination].'

- 'I was a relatively happy child during the first years at school [good beginning] ... But then school bullies destroyed my life in middle school ... This totally destroyed my sense of self-esteem and security ... I've lost the ability to trust and connect with other people [contamination].'

Why should we care about how our stories end? It turns out, as a growing number of studies reveal, that the contamination sequences – wherein good scenes are ruined and turn bad – are associated with low psychological wellbeing. In particular, the authors who write contamination stories are prone to depression and score low on self-esteem and life satisfaction.

There is also some evidence that the way we talk about our life can programme our future behaviour. In a classic study, researchers asked fifty-two couples to tell a story of how they met. In turn, those stories predicted whether the couples would divorce three years later with 94 per cent accuracy. Those who told more positive stories were more likely to stay together three years later. But those who told more negative stories about their marriage were far more likely to break up.

Why do we have this result? It is likely that the stories are not the last factor that contributed to these positive and negative outcomes. When we tell a negative story about some part of our life – like our relationships, for example – we don't restrict ourselves just to words. In fact, we also unintentionally conjure some negative memories about this event, we maintain this episode in the focus of our mind, and keep evoking negative emotions. Of course, this negativity can naturally mount up with time. It can exhaust a person and make them feel worse. So, it should perhaps come as no surprise that a contamination story could ultimately drain your mental energy and push you towards a divorce.

Try to notice whether you carry round any contamination

stories with you. All too often, we do not pay much attention to what we habitually tell other people or even ourselves. But if we want to improve our life, it would be really helpful to tune in and inspect what we're used to saying. The task is very simple: set a mental alert for the stories that turn bad. Once you detect at least one story that drags you down, you can get to work on changing it.

TRAINING GOAL:
Creating constructive stories

What does a healthy story look like then? Well, of course, there could be lots of ingredients. But as far as I am concerned, all healthy stories tend to *end constructively*.

Basically, what we need to do is to always consider how our story ends. Unhealthy stories tend to end badly or negatively (contaminating the whole narrative), while healthy stories are prone to end constructively (offering valuable experience, hope or meaning at the end).

It does not mean that a story should have a happy ending. No, not at all. But it would be helpful if the story contained at least some positive or constructive element at the end, such as your personal growth, or manifestation of agency, or finding some meaning in your suffering, getting a chance for redemption, finding communion with other people, discovering some unexpected opportunities, and so on.

As an example, let's consider so-called competence-building stories. A competence-building story can be prompted by a simple question: 'How did this failure change me for the better?'

Studies indicate that those people who construct stories of growth or competence-building rate higher for wellbeing. They report higher levels of self-esteem and life satisfaction, and rate their lives as more meaningful.

Some other studies also show that there is a link between competence-building storytelling and academic achievement. In one experiment, researchers wanted to explore whether competence-building stories could help school students to bounce back from their failures. It was revealed that those students who inserted competence-building themes in their accounts of failures showed subsequently increased levels of goal persistence and better grades, compared with their peers.

I think this makes perfect sense. Indeed, talking of one's unemployment as a story of adventure or a search for the right place feels very different from the story of one's inadequacy or global unfairness.

A simple explanation is that when you write contamination stories, you focus on your failures or adversities, and therefore you unintentionally increase and prolong your suffering. But when you make your stories constructive and highlight, let's say, how you grew or changed during this period, what happens is that you manage to appreciate the progress you have made, despite the hardships or mistakes. That way, you become much gentler on yourself and create the optimism to move forward.

PRACTICE #1:
Structure

Suppose you identify a problematic story. As a first step, it is useful to give your story some structure. Simply put, when we have a solid story structure, we can answer some of the following questions: Where does a story start? How does it progress? When does it end? What are the main events? Who are the main characters? What is the main problem or conflict?

Personally, as a useful framework, I like the concept of a story arc (also known as a narrative arc or a dramatic arc). The story arc is a great tool to establish the structure of most stories. It is widely used in storytelling and can be found in almost every book, movie, TV series, play, comic book and even video game. Not the right phrase for this context or sense, and not necessary in any case. You can think of a story arc as a formula or as a framework for writing a story.

The basic idea is that we can split a story into a number of parts or acts. There is no right answer or rule for how many acts a story should have. A story can be composed of three, five or even eight acts. It all depends on how an author wants to tell a story and the complexity of the story itself.

I prefer the five-act structure to work with our personal stories. Unless you want to create a very fancy narrative, I believe that the five-act structure is both a simple and quite comprehensive way to organise your story. As the name suggests, according to this formula, we divide a story into five acts.

Five-act story arc

Five-act story content

1. Act one (beginning): exposition	The beginning of the story and is all about setting the stage. The exposition introduces the protagonist (the hero, the main character), the secondary characters and the antagonist (the main villain), and outlines their relationships, the world they live in and the conflict that will move the story forward. Of course, nobody's life is perfect, and every protagonist is challenged by some life circumstances at the beginning of the story. Usually, there is the so-called 'inciting incident' - an event that provokes a change in the protagonist's life and creates the main problem or conflict.

2. Act two (middle): rising action	This part features the protagonist's attempts to resolve the big problem. It is marked by the so-called rising action - when tension and conflict begin to ramp up. It is common for various obstacles and complications to show up in the way. Moreover, the protagonist often loses and succumbs to doubts, fears and limitations during this stage.
3. Act three (middle): climax	Act three describes the climax or the culmination of the story. All previous events eventually lead to the climax - the worst possible moment that could happen to the protagonist. The climax is where the protagonist meets the antagonist in their final battle or confrontation. It is the point of peak tension in the story. This is where the protagonist either resolves the big problem (in the case of a happy ending) or fails to reach the goal (in the case of a tragic ending).
4. Act four (middle): falling action	This part depicts the so-called falling action. Falling action refers to events that follow the final battle and show its fallouts. The conflict begins to de-escalate, tension rapidly dissipates and life gradually gets back to normal. But the protagonist may need to 'clear up the mess' or handle some secondary issues that follow the main conflict.
5. Act five (ending): resolution	This is the end of the story and features the resolution. Resolution wraps up the narrative and fills in any missing details. Loose ends are tied up and answers to lingering questions are given. The characters celebrate with friends and reflect on their lives. We can also see how the protagonist changed due to the conflict and what his or her life looks like after the quest.

I hope that you now have a good basic understanding of what a five-act structure is all about. You may at least recognise now how a certain type of story progresses in the books you read. Or you may be able to spot different stages of storytelling in the TV shows or movies you watch. More importantly, you can also easily split any of your personal stories into different parts.

Think of a time when you faced a life challenge. It can be anything – losing in a competition, preparing for exams, working on a project, having conflict in a relationship, undergoing medical treatment, etc. Now, imagine that this situation or story is made up of three or more acts. Could you mentally picture that?

Think of what you can add to each of those acts. Act one will introduce the setting: you, the other people involved, the tone and the main problem. Act two will describe the confrontation: the hurdles on your way, the struggles, the battles, the failures, how you coped. Act five will feature the ending: the outcome, the morals, how you changed after this journey, what you plan to do next. That's all for now.

You may have a natural question: Why? Why would I do that? In essence, when you do this exercise, you take the third-person perspective. Do you remember when we zoomed out and took the third-person perspective to watch our memories from the outside (see Chapter 7)? Here, we do a similar trick. We take a look at what our story looks like from the outside, just as any real author would do.

This is a great exercise to give yourself a little bit of emotional distance. The problem with the first-person perspective – as you remember from the previous chapter – is that it immerses a person back into his or her past experiences, which can bring back negative emotions and prevent any constructive work. By contrast, the third-person perspective helps us to self-distance, to step out of any direct experience of life events. Basically, as we look at a story from the outside, we detach ourselves a bit from the events that occur in that story. As a result, we can make our feelings less intense and we can feel a little bit calmer.

In addition, this exercise helps to keep things in perspective. When we are not directly involved in certain life events, it is often much easier to remain fair with regard to those events and respond in a more adaptive way. Therefore, once you become an external observer of your own journey, you are likely to find it much easier to work on your story more consciously and constructively. For example, you can evaluate events that happen along the way, extend or shrink the content of the story, and build or redesign the structure of your narrative.

PRACTICE #2:
Write it out

As a second step, my recommendation is to actually empty your mind and write everything down. Many people underestimate the value of writing for some reason. Maybe it is because it takes more time to write than to talk about something. But you will be surprised how powerful it can be to write things down.

First of all, journaling helps to collect and better structure information about our life experiences. Many important details unavoidably get lost in our memory cellars. With writing, however, you can take your time and gradually bring all the details to the surface. One of the greatest things about this practice is that it is possible to spill out on to the page things that you didn't even know were there.

You know, it is quite common for a story to be 'shallow'. By shallow, I mean lacking information or 'filling' in the story. For example, there may be very little or no background information to tell us about the characters or the events that take place, let alone details to flesh out certain questions. A shallow character in a movie or in a book, for example, is one who we don't really get to know. We have little idea about their past, about their motivation or personality. As a result, we don't really understand why they decide to act in a certain way, we don't experience any emotional connection with them and, frankly speaking, we usually don't really care what happens to them. By the same token, a shallow story is short or very scarce in details. A person may say just a few sentences when asked to comment on some substantial topic, such as their childhood, hobbies or relationships with loved ones. 'It is okay' is a very common answer.

Journaling can definitely help to extend and enrich your narrative. There is no need to put everything down in one go. You can write as much as you want and come back as often as you want, broadening or deepening the narrative with more details. With each writing session, new details will bubble up to the surface.

Second, once you have everything written down in one place, you can do a constructive review: assess how your narrative unfolds, notice whether there are any gaps in the story, decide whether it is necessary to add more details or consider revising some parts.

Have you ever written an essay at school? I don't know about you, but I personally almost never like what I first put down on paper. I leave it, come back later, delete paragraphs, rewrite, tinker with words here and there, and add new material. This can happen literally thousands of times until I finally craft the text that I really, really like.

Honestly, I can't recall how many times I returned to this specific chapter and rewrote it, polished it, even though both my literary agent and publisher already liked it around eight months before that. Every time, I simply came up with a new idea how to make it a little bit better ... so I did.

The same approach applies to the stories about our life. If you don't like one of your narratives, you do not have to stick with it. You can come back at any point and make as many edits as you want, expanding and reshaping the plot, and reinterpreting life events in a more constructive way.

With some time, you may realise that you actually have huge control over how to shape your life experiences. You may not always control what events happen to you – whether they are good or bad, lucky or unfortunate. But you can always choose how to understand and talk about these events. You can choose, for example, how to structure your story, how many elements to add, what meanings to attach, and what conclusions to draw.

Directions

Below are some guiding questions to help you to fill in your narrative, according to a five-act structure.

Introduction
– *The theme* – What is the major theme of this story? Examples: exam preparation, job search, child-birth, relocation, self-discovery, self-expression, growth, relationships, self-isolation during the coronavirus pandemic.
– *The time* – When did this story happen?
– *The title* – How would you name this story?

Act one (exposition)
– *The place* – Where does your story take place?
– *The protagonist* – Who is the main character? What are his/her characteristics?
– *The characters* – Who are the secondary characters? What are their characteristics?
– *The problem/antagonist* – What is the main challenge or antagonist of the story? Examples:*

---

* Note that the antagonist or the main problem can have either an external or internal nature. In an external conflict, the protagonist confronts the outside force – struggling, for example, against another person, society, or the natural world. In an internal conflict, the battle occurs inside the protagonist – for example, between the protagonist and bad habits.

- External conflict: another person (e.g. boss, bully), society (e.g. culture, government, company, religion), nature (e.g. earthquake, storm, virus).
- Internal conflict: physical illness, mental issue (e.g. negative beliefs, fear, anger, bad habits, selfish impulses, addictions, loss of faith).

Act two (rising action)
– What is getting in the way?
– How does the protagonist respond to the obstacles?

Act three (climax)
– When is the climax of this story?
– How does the protagonist want the conflict to be resolved? What would an ideal scenario look like?
– What is the actual outcome? Does the protagonist reach his/her goal?

Act four (falling action)
– What are the issues that need resolving after the climax?
– How does the protagonist adjust to the new normal after the conflict?

Act five (resolution)
– How does this story end?
– How did the protagonist (a.k.a. you) change during this time?

PRACTICE #3:
Enrich the resolution

It is now time to make some tweaks to our disturbing stories. But first of all, let me ask you, how do you judge whether a story has a good ending? When does it end badly?

I find that many people attach the greatest value to the climax and focus on whether a protagonist reaches their goal or not. If the hero defeats the antagonist during their final battle, then we have a happy ending. And if the things don't go exactly as planned, and the hero is defeated, then we have a tragic ending.

Without doubt, the climax is important. We all want to overcome our initial challenges, solve problems and achieve our goals. Yet the climax is not the only factor that defines whether a story ends well.

In reality, there are many ways to make a story more constructive and positive. Below are just two ideas to consider:

Add a positive character arc	Consider whether you managed to grow in some way during the period of your story. Ask yourself: How did this period change me for the better? What qualities did I develop?
Add life opportunities	Consider what opportunities or doorways opened up during this period. Ask yourself: What is at least one good thing that happened during this period? Is there any valuable opportunity that became available during this time? Maybe you met some good people who helped you in your quest, or perhaps you had some 'me time' and could recharge your batteries.

Let's consider a character arc (or character development) in more detail as an example. A character arc is a transformation or inner change in a character over the course of a story. The term 'arc' implies the stages of a character's transformation: from the comfort zone at the beginning, up to sweeping change and tension in the middle, and then back down again to a place of comfort at the end.

The character arc

Character arc	A character arc is when a character undergoes an inner change during the story. If a story has a character arc, the character starts off his or her journey as one sort of person (with certain viewpoints and attitudes) but then they gradually transform into a different sort of person (usually through frictions and trials).
No character arc	Not all stories have a character arc. Sometimes characters don't seem to change at all. They remain with the same traits or attitudes from the beginning till the very end of the story. One reason is that authors just don't pay enough attention to the description and exploration of these characters. Characters without a character arc may often feel shallow and uninteresting.
Positive character arc	This is when a character undergoes a positive transformation. The character generally begins the story with some kind of internal flaw or weakness in their personality or behaviour (e.g. fears, negative outlook, selfishness, etc.). But as the story unfolds, the character gradually learns from their struggles, develops new qualities and ultimately becomes a better person by the end of the story.

Positive character arc (cont.)	The character may overcome some of their fears, become a bit more knowledgeable or learn to make better decisions (e.g. Bilbo Baggins in *The Hobbit*, or *There and Back Again*, by J. R. R. Tolkien).
Negative character arc	This is when a character undergoes a decline. The character may make wrong decisions, retreat deeper into their struggles or flaws, or become overwhelmed by their situation. Often enough, the character starts off good but then becomes overwhelmed by the challenges and ends up far worse off by the end than they were in the beginning (e.g. Anakin Skywalker, who turns to the dark side and becomes Darth Vader in *Star Wars: Episode III – Revenge of the Sith*).

The inner transformation of the character is triggered by the big problems or challenges that exist in the story. Let me explain. Partly, the reason why the protagonist is unable to resolve a problem or any conflict (which appears at the beginning of the story) is because he or she does not have the necessary skills yet to cope with the problem or resist the forces of the antagonist. So, if the protagonist wants to resolve the current problem, he or she must change or evolve in some way, acquiring new skills and abilities. At some point, the protagonist starts to reflect more about the situation, sometimes coming to terms with their weaknesses. Ideally, the character starts to learn and change in response to the conflict and difficult circumstances, getting a better chance to deal with the same problem in a different storyline. Otherwise, the character will relive the same psychodrama time and time again.

A character arc is one of the greatest factors in defining

the success of any story. Let's imagine a protagonist who fails to reach their big goal but nevertheless comes out as a better person at the end of the story. They may have overcome some of their weaknesses, become a bit more knowledgeable, or developed more resilience, and so forth. Is this a good ending? Definitely!

Sometimes character development is even more important than goal achievement and climax victories. Simply put, if the character manages to grow, it is something that can make thousands of other victories possible in the future.

Believe me, failing to reach a goal does not make your story bad, nor does it make you a loser. Let's be realistic. We can't always hit the mark. Some goals require more attempts, more time, more skills, while other goals are simply unachievable (through no fault of our own). But what makes a story really bad is when the character fails to grow or change in some way. Why? Because this sets you up to have difficulties and problems in the future. A character who does not grow is the character who is doomed to repeat the same mistakes or to experience the same problems over and over again.

The goal of this exercise is not to fool yourself that bad things are actually good. No! If you did not reach your goal at the climax scene, you should admit this fact. We should always remain honest with ourselves.

The goal of this exercise is to try to extend your original narrative a bit. Life is rarely either black or white. There is always room for both the negatives and the positives in any tale, in any movie, or in most life events. Even if things don't turn out as planned, it does not mean that every single moment during this period of time was terrible.

I simply encourage you to mine your experience thoroughly and examine whether there was anything positive (or constructive) along the way or as a result of those circumstances. If there wasn't, that's fine. But if there was a silver lining, why not acknowledge it?

That way you remain honest with yourself, but you also make your story more comprehensive, more balanced, and much more empowering. Moreover, the more details the story has, the more it reflects the truth.

So the next time the sky falls in, don't rush to beat yourself up. Don't rush to declare yourself a failure. Pause. Take a deep breath. And get your words right.

Examples

Let's assume that you're writing a story about a secret crush. You've liked someone for a long time but always felt anxious about making a move. So, you define the climax as the moment when you finally ask your crush on a date. This is the turning point of this story. And, of course, we all hope that she or he will say: 'Yes, I'd love to!' But let's imagine that the ideal scene never happens. Even worse, it turns out to be a 'disaster' – you get turned down rudely in front of your peers.

How would you end this story? A catastrophe? Filled with embarrassment? Full of bitterness? It is very tempting to do so, I know. But it does not have to be like that. Though you did not reach your goal, you may recognise how much you changed during this period of time. You may discover that you actually worked up the courage to ask your crush on a date, which was a dreadful experience at the beginning of this narrative. As a matter of fact, you developed the strength to face your fears, which will help you to make a move again in the future and find a perfect match. Believe it or not, you upgraded to the Protagonist 2.0. version. Is this a good ending? I think so.

In the table below, I list some examples to give you a better idea of how to enrich the resolution of some stories. The first column outlines the original narratives that contain contamination – the bad endings. The second column includes a new constructive sequence that we add to enrich and extend the original narrative.

Examples that feature a positive character arc

Original story	Extended story (feat. personal growth)
Mike was bullied at school. He says that this negative experience made him extremely insecure.	Five years later, Mike decided to learn how to protect himself and others by learning martial arts.
Oliver had been preparing for an important tennis tournament for months. But during the first match, he sprained his ankle and had to withdraw from the tournament.	Oliver added more stretching exercises in his training to minimise the chances of the same trauma in the future.
When Matt was young, his grandfather died, which caused a lot of suffering for the young boy.	With time, Matt realised that it is important to seize the day and appreciate the moments of closeness with family and those who are around.

Original story	Extended story (feat. personal growth)
Parents were neglecting and abusing Molly in her childhood.	Molly developed a high level of empathy because of her traumatic experience and came to value good human connections in her adult relationships.
Josh could not find a decent job for almost two years after graduating from a top university - and, as a result, felt like a complete failure.	During this time, Josh discovered that he just wanted to have a prestigious job so that he could have a big pay packet at the end of the month, but he did not actually know what kind of job would be internally satisfying for him.

Examples that feature life opportunities

Original story	Extended story (feat. life opportunities)
During the pandemic lockdown, Frank struggled with staying at home and was worried that he might be laid off.	Frank realised that he had more time to read and spend time with his kids.
Martha was diagnosed with cancer and had to undergo surgery and a long period of treatment.	Martha was grateful that all her family united during this challenging time and showed support and care.
Eve lost a maths competition.	Eve found new friends during the competition.

Visual summary

Common problem:
Contamination
stories

Training goal:
Creating
constructive stories

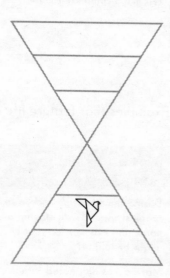

—————— **Chapter summary** ——————

- Storytelling takes up a significant part of our life and can have a great impact on our mental wellbeing and behaviour.

- Self-stories and stories about our life have a particular power. They can build you up or take you down; they can either expand life or narrow it dramatically.

- Contamination stories are stories that start good but turn bad at the end. Contamination stories are associated with negative outcomes for mental health and behaviour.

- Constructive stories refer to stories that have a constructive or positive element at the end, such as personal growth, communion, redemption, or life opportunities.

- It is possible to make tweaks to, edit or rewrite our stories.

- Visualise a problematic story split into different acts. For example, you can use the three- or five-act structure.

- Write down the problematic story and organise information using the five-act story structure. Use the guiding questions to fill your narrative.

- Enrich the story resolution by adding a character arc or life opportunities. Identify at least one way this period helped you to build your own character and become better in some way. How did you become stronger or smarter because of the event that transpired?

10

Master of Behaviour

Habit is a behaviour that we perform automatically, with minimal conscious awareness. Brushing your teeth in the morning, greeting people on the phone, smoking, and even walking, are all examples of habits.

More technically, a habit is a memory (procedural memory) of what you're supposed to do when you face a particular situation. If you do something in a certain context or situation, your brain gradually learns the association between the situation (the cue) and the action (the behaviour). So when the situation is encountered again, the behaviour is performed automatically.

Let's draw a line between controlled actions and automatic actions (habits). Not all of our actions are automatic – that's important to remember. Many of our actions are conscious and controlled by our reason. But if you repeat a certain action over and over again, eventually it can become habitual.

Consider driving a car as an example. When you drove a car for the first time, you thought about each tiny step – how to follow the lines, how to turn, how to pull over. Then you drove again – making mistakes but also memorising how to do it right. And then again – remembering how you did it the last time. With every new attempt, you become more skilful and think less about each tiny step. And before long, you can drive like a pro, being able to think of some other, unrelated stuff while you steer and control the car.

To sum up, we make conscious choices at first, but then they become automatic with time and practice. Basically, you do not have to give any conscious thought to how to perform a habit because you've repeated this behaviour many times before. All you have to do is pull this behaviour from your memory storage (procedural memory).

According to one study from Duke University in Durham, North Carolina, habits constitute around 40 per cent of our daily actions. That is, we perform getting on for half of our daily activities not because of conscious thoughts and decisions but because of habit. This is an absolutely staggering number. Think about it. Almost half of our actions are automatic.

Take a moment and think of behaviours you do automatically. For example, how often do you pick up your phone and browse the news during the day? Do you often consciously think to yourself *I should get my phone and check my social networks?'* Of course not. It normally happens on autopilot.

In a similar vein, thousands of other actions are habit-driven. We wake up more or less at the same time every day, we brush our teeth, take a shower and get dressed. Then we put the kettle on, make breakfast, drink coffee and drive along familiar routes to work. Again, how often do you think about the steps involved in brushing your teeth? Or putting your clothes on? Or making a cup of coffee? Even when we drive familiar routes, we don't think much about the directions, where to go and when to turn. We just do it.

Habits, in this context, play an important role in simplifying our everyday life. On the one hand, habits allow you to perform an action without being conscious of every step. Just imagine how difficult it would be to live if you had to think consciously about every action you perform. Your mind would simply blow up from overload. The huge benefit of habits is that you don't have to think about how to do a routine action – you just do it.

On the other hand, habits free up your thinking so that you can focus on other tasks. You can basically be more clear-headed. While you carry out some habits on autopilot, your reason can either rest or be used for some higher-level activities. For example, while washing the dishes after dinner, you may think, let's say, about how to spend your weekends, or how to write a good essay for your class, or what movie to watch in the evening.

It should also be noted that habits are normally very resistant to decay. The procedural memory tends to last for years. Since you've performed a behaviour repeatedly, it gets hardwired, in a sense, in your brain. Most people, for example, can hop on a bike and ride it smoothly even if they have not done this since childhood.

For this reason, habits are also very difficult to break. As you've probably heard before: *old habits die hard*. If you want to reverse a firmly entrenched habit on purpose, it can be notoriously hard to do it. That's why there are so many people who struggle to change their routines and who keep coming back to their old habits again and again.

Moreover, even if you manage to kick an old habit, it is easy to fall back into it. Let's assume you used to smoke and you stopped for five years. But one day you're at a party, having fun, drinking beer, and all a sudden you ask: 'Could I have a cigarette?' You simply default to behaviour that you did a lot in the past.

In most cases, it is really good that habits are long-lived kind of memories. After all, we are able to perform a certain skill even after going years without practice. It would probably be very annoying if we forgot our skills quickly and had to relearn the same thing over and over again.

COMMON PROBLEM:
Bad habits

Not all habits serve us well. The category of habits that can harm your health or prevent you from achieving your goals is known as bad or unhealthy habits. It could be smoking a pack of cigarettes, even though you understand that it harms your lungs. Or it could be checking your Instagram every two minutes when you should be working.

Generally, these are the repetitive behaviours that we don't find useful. They keep us stuck and make us do things that we do not really want to do. You may want to become a person who wakes up early in the morning, for example, but instead you keep hitting snooze on your alarm every time.

The most dangerous habits, of course, are those that may

have serious long-term health implications. Researchers usually agree that the most harmful habits include drinking sugary beverages, eating processed food, staying sedentary for a prolonged period of time, smoking, binge drinking and taking drugs. All of these behaviours are significant factors in major illnesses such as obesity, diabetes, cancer, addiction and heart problems.

There are, of course, bad habits that are relatively benign, such as mindless scrolling on your phone, being late, or biting your nails. Yet these behaviours are still referred to as bad habits because they have a negative impact on your attention and productivity. According to surveys, people spend on average three hours and fifteen minutes on their phones every day. In addition, people pick up and check their phones on average fifty-eight times a day. Now just think how many things you could have done or achieved if you had used this time more productively instead?

All everyday habits may seem small and innocent. But the problem is that the effects of small things add up. This means that falling back on bad habits every day can add up to something really nasty. Spending three hours a day on your phone, for example, does not seem to be a big deal in itself. But a quick scroll here, browsing there – and you've already used ninety hours a month. By the same token, there is no serious damage if you eat something unhealthy once in a while. But if you make a dietary mistake every day, you significantly increase your chances of having health problems later in life.

Again, nobody is perfect. We all carry out unhealthy behaviours from time to time. But if you find yourself repeating these unhealthy behaviours, it is a smart idea to stop this practice in its tracks before it turns into a routine. It is unlikely that you want to get stuck with an unhealthy habit, which would be very hard to chip away at. As Warren Buffett once said: 'Chains of habit are too light to be felt until they are too heavy to be broken.'

TRAINING GOAL:
Building good habits

While some habits can set you back, there are many that are great to have. Habits that are beneficial to your health and bring you closer to your goals are known as good, helpful or healthy habits.

Every one of us has a large repertoire of helpful habits that we carry out every day – washing up, taking a shower, getting dressed, doing laundry, making breakfast, sorting rubbish, driving, reading emails, stretching, turning off the lights when we leave a room, and so on.

Let's mention habits that are good for our health, first of all. Learning to brush our teeth when we were young, for example, helps to keep our teeth healthy. Learning to fasten a seatbelt helps to prevent us from injuries and death in case of a car accident.

Some habits come with a bunch of benefits. Research has shown, for example, that regular exercise can improve mental health (by relieving anxiety, stress and depression) and reduce risks of chronic diseases (heart disease, stroke, diabetes and cancer). It can strengthen bones and muscles, improve memory and thinking, lead to better sleep, improve your sex life and increase the chances of living longer.

There is no magic here. The fact is that the small actions we choose to do every day add up over time. Healthy behaviours you do every day add up to a longer and disease-free life.

But it is not only about health. Good habits also underlie professional achievements. If you do something over and over again in a certain field, you develop your skills, hone your craft, and can eventually showcase outstanding results.

Great results are rarely, if ever, achieved all at once. People become good at their chosen discipline because they take regular actions. An athlete can set a world record because he or she trains many hours a week. An artist can create a masterpiece because he or she practises every day.

If you want to run a marathon, for example, you probably won't sign up for the first upcoming race without the proper training. It normally takes a long period of preparation, a careful diet, a programme of progressively longer runs and building mental toughness. A marathon is a physical ordeal, and if your body is not prepared, running a marathon may send you to hospital.

If you dream about becoming a footballer, for example, you can't do it overnight. You will start with something basic like, for example, kicking a ball. It will then take months to build many proper habits – be it how to pass, how to chip, how to bend the ball, how to shoot with power, how to dribble, and so on. It may then take years to polish and develop your habits, which leads to mastery. Professional football players, for example, never stop improving their technique during their career. This is one of the reasons why they can exhibit excellence and 'create magic' on the pitch during a match.

As Aristotle once said: 'We are what we repeatedly do. Excellence, then, is not an act, but a habit.' I couldn't agree more. Many professional athletes would agree with this thought as well. As Bruce Lee famously noted: 'I fear not the man who has practised 10,000 kicks once, but I fear the man who has practised one kick 10,000 times.'

Before we get any further, I want to make it clear that this chapter will not give guidance on how to get rid of any addictive behaviours, such as smoking, gambling or any substance addiction. These kinds of habits are usually very deep-seated. And changing such habits may sometimes require professional assistance. So, if you are struggling to quit a bad habit, it is good to remember that you may benefit from working with a mental health professional. Yet, if you want to understand how to cope with trivial bad habits – such as oversleeping, being disorganised, being too sedentary, eating fast food, consuming too much sugar, swearing, and so on – this chapter can help a lot.

The easiest strategy at our disposal is to focus on building good habits. If you incorporate new healthy behaviours in your life, you can simply replace or marginalise your existing bad habits.

For example, if you want to cut down on sugary soft drinks, instead of struggling and suppressing the urges, you could try making yourself a glass of carbonated water with a thin slice of lemon (if this works for you). Or if you have a hard time waking up early in the morning and constantly battle with the snooze button, the easiest strategy is to train yourself to go to bed much earlier in the evening to get enough sleep.

Anyway, whatever your goal is, when you work with behaviour, instead of trying to stop doing something, it is more productive to focus on how you can build new healthy behaviours. And that's what we are going to learn next.

PRACTICE #1:
Establish a cue

Every habit starts with a cue. A cue is a stimulus that triggers you to perform a behaviour. It can be anything that reminds you to take action. Or, to put it differently, it can be anything that you associate with performing a specific action.

Cues can take lots of different forms. They could be any external stimulus, such as an event (e.g. the buzzing of a mobile phone), a time of day (e.g. immediately after waking up), physical items (e.g. trainers, a pack of cigarettes), people around you, preceding actions, sounds, smells, etc. Or they could be any internal stimulus, like your physical state (e.g. a drop in blood sugar), an emotional state (e.g. feeling anxious), a thought, etc.

So, to establish a habit, we first need to place a visible cue in our environment that would remind us to perform a behaviour. Want to drink more water? You can, for example, fill a jug with water and put it on your desktop. The jug will serve as a cue, reminding you to have a glass of water during the day.

Examples
- *Drink more water* – Keep a jug of water on your table.
- *Read every day* – Place a book on your bedside table.

- *Eat more healthily* – Keep a bowl of apples on the kitchen table (or in any visible spot around the home or office).
- *Jog in the evening* – Place your trainers in the hallway in plain sight.
- *Hit the gym after work* – Join a gym that is on your way home from work or close to home.

The basic idea is that by tweaking our environment, we can make the preferred behaviour a little bit easier. How so?

First off, a cue acts as a reminder to perform a certain behaviour. When the relevant cues are put in the right spots in our environment, we don't need to think about a new habit throughout the day. As a result, we don't forget to perform the habit and we also manage to save mental energy.

Second, environment tends to nudge people to act in a certain way. Especially if our willpower and motivation are down, we're more likely to make decisions based on what we have around us. If we're tired or sick, for example, very few of us will make an extra effort to go to a shop, look for the necessary products and cook a healthy meal for dinner. No, most people will pick whatever is in front of them.

These are just some of the reasons why it is important not to leave cues to chance. If you shape the environment where you live or work, then the environment will shape your behaviour, prompting you to make better and healthy choices. You can, for example, put a yoga mat in the living room if you want to exercise more; or you can turn off the social media notifications on your phone and computer if you want to concentrate on your work during the day. And these triggers will make it much easier for you to engage and follow through, even when you're tired or reluctant to stick to a habit.

PRACTICE #2:
Start small

Some people believe that if they go big, starting at their highest level, they will achieve the result faster. For example, a common picture I see in the gym is when a beginner goes in and attempts to lift the entire gym on his first day, picking too-heavy weights or performing tons of exercises for all muscle groups. At best, this leads to a quick burnout – it does not feel good when all your body is in pain after a workout. At worst, it is possible to end up with serious injuries.

Instead, it is a much wiser solution to make your new behaviour as easy as possible. And the best way to make your behaviour easy is to start small. I mean really, really stupid-small. You take a behaviour you want to perform and shrink it, so that it no longer feels like a challenge. Alternatively, you take a behaviour and shrink it to the point it becomes impossible not to do it. Want to meditate regularly, for example? Meditate just for one minute every day. That's it.

Examples
- *Exercise more* – Rather than doing thirty squats, do two. That's it.
- *Get up earlier* – Don't force yourself to get up one hour earlier. Start by rising five minutes earlier.

- *Eat more vegetables* – Aim to eat just one small carrot (or whatever you like) per day.
- *Read more* – Read for only five minutes a day.
- *Engage in small-talk more* – Rather than forcing yourself to start a conversation, start by saying just 'Hi' or smiling once a day.

It is completely okay if you feel that this all seems very trivial or slow, or that you can do more. It just means that you are doing it right. It is important to remember that we're not training our stamina here, but trying to build a habit. Given this, the point is not to do the things you can do, but to do the things you can *sustain*.

Let's say you want to be able to run a marathon. Where would you start? Running five, ten miles? Running as much as you can every day? That's where many people go into overdrive and then get burned out. If one mile is currently your best result, how can you expect to show the best of yourself every time now? Do it for a week in a row, and you will soon find yourself exhausted, frustrated and increasingly wanting to trade your exercise time for TV time.

Starting small is great at least for two reasons. First off, it is almost a guarantee that you will perform a behaviour. There is a simple principle: the harder the behaviour is to do, the less likely people will do it. And conversely, the easier the behaviour is to do, the more likely people will do it. It is not a secret that difficult tasks often appear daunting. It takes longer to complete them and they quickly deplete our strength and become overwhelming. That's why trying to make changes way too fast, or ones that are way too big, is a recipe for a disaster. If the task is too big, people get tired, feel demoralised and soon resist any further action. But if you make your behaviour really small, it becomes really hard not to do it. If all you have to do is one squat or run for three minutes, you will laugh at the challenge, right? Think about it. Everyone can do one squat.

Second, starting small also provides an immediate pay-off. When we set a goal and get what we want, we feel great. Our brain releases dopamine, which is known as a 'feel good' neurotransmitter that creates the sense of pleasure. The trick is that it does not matter how big a goal is. Even when you set a really small goal and achieve it, such as running for five minutes, you can still receive a spike in dopamine. And each time your brain gets a new dose of this rewarding chemical, it will make you want to repeat the behaviour.

The most important thing is to start; the rest is the downhill race. Over time, small steps compound and add up to a big and positive change. As you do your tiny habit consistently, you will gradually improve. If you start with a five-minute run, you will want to increase it to six minutes in a week. If you start with three push-ups, soon you will find yourself upgrading to five push-ups, then ten, twenty, thirty, and so on.

Just don't complicate the routine too quickly. Learning to be patient is probably the most important skill here. If you add too much too soon, you risk making the habit difficult and falling off the wagon. The goal is to resist the temptation to do more and add fewer than you can expect to handle. It will feel much more manageable, more welcome, more comfortable, and will have a huge impact in the long run.

PRACTICE #3:
Stay consistent

What do we hear most often when we learn a new skill? What would your tutor or coach say during a class? Practise, practise and practise! It will perhaps not come as a surprise that practice is the necessary element for forming a habit.

I hate to break it to you, but forming new habits is quite a slow process and doesn't happen overnight. Procedural memories (habits) require much more time to get recorded in our brain and muscles than any other type of memory. Just as a comparison, it may take less than a minute to learn a new fact (semantic memory) and around two months to build a simple habit (procedural memory).

Basically, habits result from the mechanism called over-learning – when we do the activity often and for a long period of time. Anatomically, when a certain action is performed, certain neural pathways in the brain that are needed to perform this action are activated. Every time you repeat an action, you activate the same neural pathways (synapses) over and over again. With repeated activation, these neural pathways get stronger and begin to work faster and more efficiently. As a result, the brain can emit the practised behaviour quicker, more automatically and more skilfully.

The time frame for forming a habit is pretty wide. You may see all kinds of answers floating around on the internet and in research literature: a week, a month, a year. According to a UCL study, it takes on average sixty-six days (two months) to pick up a new habit. Yet the research also points out that although the median time is sixty-six days, the time frame can range from eighteen to 254 days for a habit to stick.

It all depends on the complexity of the habit, the circumstances and the person themselves. As you'd imagine, doing five squats per day may become habitual pretty fast. By contrast, if you normally wake up at 9 a.m., learning to wake up at 5 a. m. every day would probably take more time and dedication.

Your best bet is to aim for at least two months to build a relatively simple habit. It is helpful to remember that building a habit is more like running a marathon, not a sprint.

But don't get discouraged if it takes longer than that. Eventually, even the most challenging of behaviours can become automated. Think of learning to drive a car. It takes months to learn the traffic rules, then months of anxious driving in the streets, and sometimes years, before we can drive calmly and skilfully on autopilot.

The bottom line is: all you have to do is to keep going. The behaviour needs to be repeated regularly before it will record in your brain as a habit. The more often you repeat an action, the faster you will keep it as a habit.

How can we make this process easier and more fun? I believe that the most helpful tool is to get a calendar to track your progress. Any physical 365-day calendar that you can hang on your wall will do. Alternatively, it can be a calendar in your notebook or laptop.

In the left-hand column, we list the habits we want to be working on. The columns on the right contain days of the week – from Monday till Sunday. The exercise is very simple. You just mark each day with big red X on the calendar when you perform the routine.

Habit tracker example

	Mon	Tue	Wed	Thu	Fri	Sat	Sun
Gym workout	X	-	X	-	X	-	-
Drink 1.5 litres of water	X	X	X	X	X	-	-
Stretching	-	-	-	-	X	-	-

First of all, the habit tracker allows us to visualise our progress. With each passing day, we can see how much progress we've already made. We can see, for example, that this person went to gym three times last week. He also drank enough water during the working days. But he stretched only once, on Friday.

Second, the habit tracker actually motivates us to repeat the behaviour. The trick here is that the habit tracker draws on the so-called consistency bias. In short, people like being consistent. The more energy we invest in doing something, the more committed we tend to be to it. If you engage with a behaviour for at least a couple of weeks, for example, it is very likely that you will feel an extra drive to continue doing this routine. The chain of X marks on the calendar will get longer, you will want to remain consistent, your motivation will be boosted, and you will keep going.

The main goal here is to make sure that we repeat the behaviour regularly. If you want to exercise more, for example, try to do it at the same time and at the same place for two months. You wake up at 7 a.m., for example, exercise for ten minutes, and go about your business. You wake up the next day at 7 a.m., exercise for ten minutes again, and go about your business. And before you know it, you have a new habit – this routine will become so automated that you won't be thinking about it any more, you will just do it.

Of course, we all may accidentally skip a day sometimes. We may oversleep, feel overwhelmed or simply forget. The good news is that your efforts don't go wasted if you take a day off. Even top performers make slip-ups and fall off track occasionally. If you slip for one day, just bounce back and continue the practice.

The last thing that I want to suggest is not to add too many habits to your habit tracker at once. The more habits you add, the harder it will be to do all of them. I personally tend to work on just one habit at a time. Once I finish with this habit – when it becomes a natural part of my life – I remove it from my calendar and add a new behaviour to track.

Visual summary

Common problem:
Bad habits

Training goal:
Building good habits

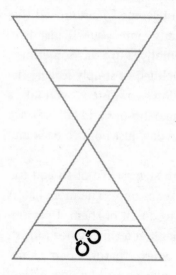

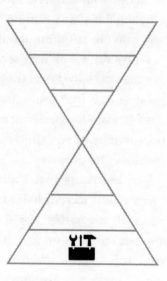

───────── **Chapter summary** ─────────

- Habits are automatic behaviours that you do regularly without thinking about them.
- Bad habits are those habits that harm your health and keep you away from achieving your goals.
- Good habits are those habits that are beneficial to your health and help you to accomplish your goals.
- Habits are normally very resistant to decay. The procedural memory tends to last for years.
- The easiest strategy is to focus on building up new healthy habits that could eventually replace bad habits, rather than trying just to stop unwanted behaviour.

Part Three

Visual summary

Common problems: Emotional overwhelm, contamination stories, bad habits

Training goals: Improve emotional regulation, create constructive stories, build good habits

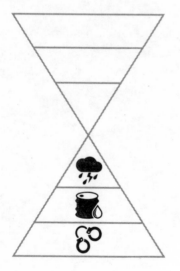

	Common problem	Training goal	Practice
4. Emotions	Emotional overwhelm	Improve emotional regulation	1) Label 2) Breath 3) Investigate
5. Words	Contamination stories	Creating constructive stories	1) Structure 2) Write it out 3) Enrich
6. Behaviour	Bad habits	Building good habits	1) Establish a cue 2) Start small 3) Stay consistent

You can also do the aforementioned exercises digitally with the help of the Brightway journaling app. You can download the app free at www.brightway.app, from the App Store or from Google Play. There is also a 'How to Use the App' page at the end of this book for more information.

Part Four

The Way to
Personal Mastery

11

Walking the Path

HOW TO GET STARTED

There are many different martial arts, and most of them have a ranking or grading system. Most people, even those who don't practise combat sports, have heard of the term 'black belt' and understand that it represents a high level of skill. But few know that there are many other belt colours and rankings.

There is no such thing as a black belt in mixed martial arts (MMA) or integrative self-care. In MMA, generally, the training process is less formalised, compared with the traditional martial arts schools.

But this does not mean that you can't benefit from the concept of a grading system. We've gone over many techniques in this book, and there are many more to learn elsewhere. But it is always important to move step by step (to avoid informational overload and actually be able to learn something).

So, just to give your training process some structure, the

concept of the grading system may prove useful. Try to imagine that you test for some ranks and belts as you progress with integrative self-care. I'll let you decide for yourself what this grading system may look like for you personally.

Let's assume that, in learning how to deal with your emotions, you mastered the 'label' technique. And right now, you can name and distinguish what you feel, rather than ignoring or suppressing your negative emotions. My congratulations! You got your first belt! Please carry on.

According to the Pyramid Model, there are six main levels where you can achieve mastery. There is no one way to start. And there is no one right way. You can start at any level, whatever you find easier or more important. Start with one level. Learn the suggested techniques. Imagine that you were awarded a specific belt and rank. Celebrate it. And then move on to the next level.

This book does not cover everything, but it provides the fundamentals. If there were such a thing as a black belt in integrative self-care, and you mastered all techniques and skills described in this book, you'd definitely get your black belt. Below are a few examples of how to get started.

STARTING WITH THOUGHTS

If you were conscious during 2020–2022 and beyond, chances are that you experienced more negative self-talk and anxiety than ever. In challenging times, like the COVID-19 pandemic, it is very easy to get caught up in negative thoughts. You may have concerns about safety, worries about financial security, or just feel uncertain about how life is going to change or when it will return to normal. It is absolutely understandable to feel this way. And the concerns about the pandemic are valid. That said, during the pandemic or any other life-threatening situation, we may also be having lots of unhelpful and exaggerated thoughts such as *We're all going to die* or *There is nothing I can do*, which can make our feelings more intense and make it hard to cope with the situation.

Josh was one of the millions of people who started feeling unsettled when the pandemic broke out in 2020. His propensity to worry skyrocketed. The feelings of fear and anxiety built up until they eventually exploded.

When Josh came to ask for a piece of advice about where to start his self-care practice, I asked whether he'd like to examine his thought patterns, given the fact that Josh had a very analytical mindset, doing data analysis for a living. Josh was very excited to find out that his research skills could prove useful for self-care and started to learn cognitive techniques.

The first step was to catch what kind of thoughts Josh was experiencing. Below is an example of the thought record that Josh used.

Date	Situation	Emotions	Thoughts
Sept 2020	There is a COVID-19 pandemic right now.	Feeling anxious, afraid, stressed, frustrated.	– Lots of people are getting sick and dying. – My parents are not safe. – There is no way I can protect my family.

The second step was to examine the credibility of those thoughts around the pandemic. At this stage, we put each thought on trial, one at a time, and explored different ways of looking at the situation. Below is an example of analysing the thought 'There is no way I can protect my family'.

Thought	Evidence for	Evidence against	Verdict
There is no way I can protect my family.	The risk of infection is high. People can spread the virus even without symptoms, so it is impossible to tell who is sick.	There are safety measures that can help: wearing a face mask, washing hands, using a hand sanitiser, social distancing, self-isolation. A vaccine is being produced.	Although COVID-19 creates real risks, there are some things I can do to protect my family and reduce the risk of infection.

Keeping a thought record proved to be an effective way to start self-care practice. Though the situation remained difficult, and it was actually getting worse every week, Josh managed to stop his spiral of negative thinking and found some inner peace.

But it was only a part of the story. After surviving a few waves of lockdown, and getting vaccinated, Josh found himself confident enough not to wear a face mask in public.

After getting two doses of vaccine, he no longer had any worries of getting coronavirus. After all, the studies indicated almost 95 per cent efficacy of some vaccines. However, in six months, Josh got sick. He had mild symptoms but still was not feeling well, having a cough, fever and then weakness for a few weeks.

After this, Josh decided to do his research again.

Date	Situation	Emotions	Thoughts
Aug 2021	Stopped wearing a face mask in crowded and enclosed spaces.	Feeling confident, optimistic.	The family and I are fully vaccinated. We are safe now.

Compared to the first case, Josh found a few positive thoughts in his thought record, rather than just negative ones. But this does not mean that a positive thought is always good and cannot be put on trial. Below, you can see the analysis of the thought *We are safe now*.

Thought	Evidence for	Evidence against	Verdict
The family and I are fully vaccinated. We are safe now.	Vaccines are reported to be effective at preventing infection, serious illness and death (including from the Delta variant, which is more contagious than other variants).	Since the available vaccines are not 100 per cent effective at preventing infection, some people who are fully vaccinated can still get infected (especially after some time). Vaccinated people can also spread the virus to others.	We can safely gather indoors with people who are also fully vaccinated. But to reduce the risk of being infected and prevent spreading the virus to others, I should continue wearing a mask in public settings.

A lot of people hear the phrase 'manage your thoughts' and assume it means thinking positively. It should be noted that the opposite of an unhelpful thought is a realistic thought, rather than a positive one.

I have nothing against positive thinking and often encourage it. That said, it is good to know that positive thinking can encourage optimistic bias (or unrealistic optimism). This is when a person overestimates the probability of experiencing positive events, which leads to risky behaviours. Furthermore, when things don't work out as planned, we end up feeling frustrated and distressed.

The bottom line is: overly negative and overly positive thinking are just two extremes. Both of them can easily lead us astray. This is especially relevant in the context of a global pandemic. On the one hand, you can be consumed with thoughts about getting sick and feel terrified to ever go out and meet other people. On the other hand, you may accept the best-case scenario, being overly optimistic that that you will be always totally fine, which may turn out to be a huge disappointment.

STARTING WITH MEMORIES

Meet Jessica, twenty-seven years old, who started to do a monthly review during the pandemic as part of her self-care practice. Here is her report for March 2021:

Category	What went well?	What did not go so well?	What could be improved?
Health/ fitness	Learned a new yoga pose (revolved triangle pose).	Putting on weight during lockdown. Lack of cardio exercises.	It is getting warmer outside, so I can go out jogging while gyms are closed.
Job	The team was praised by CTO for good work.	Frank was offered a position at another company and will leave in two months.	We need to start looking for a good replacement.

Category	What went well?	What did not go so well?	What could be improved?
Family	Emily came over to visit. We had a lovely dinner with the whole family at the restaurant nearby.	Since Emily has relocated, I see her less often.	I want to remain close to my sister, no matter how far away she is now. I shall build a routine to call or text her at weekends.
Friendship	I started to realise that a balance is more important than being focused just on career.	I sacrificed my social life too much to realise my career ambitions.	I will set aside time each week to catch up with friends (once lockdown is over). I will also check in more regularly (e.g. texting on social media).

After a few months of review practice, Jessica gained her first major insight into how her life was organised. As she says: 'I've realised lately that I have not paid adequate or regular attention to my social life ... I used to spend too much time in the office and hardly any time with those I love ... It never felt like a problem, to tell you the truth ... Maybe because there were still people around in the workspace ... But the last couple of months of self-isolation were tough ... I've been feeling lonelier since the lockdown ... especially on nights when you sit down and realise that it is just you and the TV in the room ... Something just did not feel right ...'

There is a famous quote: 'The truth will set you free, but first it will piss you off.' I guess it applies to Jessica's situation. It does not feel good, for sure, to realise that your life is not perfect. But once we comprehend the harsh truth, we can also understand what needs to be changed or fixed to improve the situation. For example, feeling disappointed that she once made a trade-off, Jessica decided to reorganise her life priorities. While still wanting to build a successful career, she was now determined to carve out more time for things that proved to be more important, such as relationships and leisure time.

STORY #1:
My journey of writing The Pyramid Mind

If you don't want to start with the level of your memories or thoughts, another option is to start with your words. Below, I will give you two examples from my personal life that illustrate how you can work on your life stories.

The first story is about the period in which I wrote this book. It does not include all the details or events that happened during that period, as I don't want to overwhelm you with unnecessary information. It is just an overview. But it will give you an idea of how I structured and worked on this narrative.

Introduction
Writing a book takes lots of time, not to mention effort. And whether an author recognises it or not, the process of writing – how the author lives through this period – is a story in its own right. Just like any other story, it has a beginning, a

middle and an ending. There are also ups and downs that occur during this time, there are allies and antagonists who either help in your endeavours or put obstacles in the way. There are moments of doubt, victories, the feelings of success or failure, and, of course, the opportunities for self-reflection and personal growth.

I was able to structure this particular story almost from the very beginning. I had no idea what events would take place in the process, what I would experience, how I would cope, or how this story would unfold and eventually end up. But it was easy for me to understand the main parts and elements of this journey almost from day one. Mainly, this is because it is not my first book. I have previously worked with academic publishers, and therefore I expected that the work on a non-fiction book would be similar in some ways.

Act one (exposition)

- Inciting incident: this story starts with signing a book contract with my UK publisher and preparation for the writing (i.e. the preparation for the quest).
- Characters: me, my literary agent, publisher, family, friends.
- The main challenge: the challenge is to get through and ultimately create a great book that would be valuable to people.

Act two (rising action)

Act two is all about the writing process itself and its main obstacles. I will mention just two challenges that I experienced during this period.

Challenge one (insomnia) – From time to time, I experienced negative self-talk related to my writing. If I crafted a section that was not good enough, I instantly experienced negative chatter somewhere at the back of my mind. And it would not shut up. That 'inner enthusiast' did not shut up even in the middle of the night, sometimes leading to sleepless nights. I did not have a good sleep for a couple of months, because my mental gears continued grinding at night, keeping me awake.

Solution: quite similar techniques that helped Josh to overcome his worries about the pandemic proved to be effective in coping with my nightly nagging mental chatter. It turned out that most of the time it was enough just to write down everything that bothered me on a piece of paper before going to bed and return to those notes the next morning. This way, I was basically able to declutter my mind and let it rest at night.

Challenge two (doubts) – As tension was rising, more negative thoughts began appearing in my head, bombarding my self-confidence: *What if this book is actually horrible? What if nobody reads it? There are so many great books in the libraries about which nobody has ever heard. You spent so many years on this project, what if it was just a waste of time? Maybe I should have chosen an easier path.*

Solution: I wrote down all these negative thoughts as they appeared and then actively challenged all of them, one by one. The most important thing here is not to delay this practice. The faster you identify and challenge your negative thoughts, the faster you can restore peace of mind.

Act three (climax)

Act three features the last three months of the writing-up period. I personally understood the climax scene as the book delivery date (the deadline).

Big challenge (exhaustion) – Subjectively, this was the hardest time of the writing. I was already mentally and physically exhausted but had to keep pushing and polishing the manuscript. Even though I love writing, each morning started with the thought of how I would find shelter on some distant island far, far away. Even the simplest of tasks felt like a mountain to climb during those days.

Act four (falling action)

The falling action is mainly about what happened after the book delivery. It involves receiving comments from the publisher, revising, making corrections, working on the illustrations and preparing for the book release.

Act five (resolution)

Act five describes the period when the book is published, celebration with loved ones, reflection on the path, and unexpected events that happen afterwards (that may lead to a new story).

Ideally, act five should include some constructive elements. As you remember, these are positive things or good outcomes that you can identify and insert at the end of your story.

Many people consider the outcomes post factum – when a story is already over, and it is time to reflect on the whole path. But if you work on a story consciously and creatively, there are actually no rules for when or how you can shape act five. You can do it at any point, even at the very beginning of the story. You are the author of your stories, don't forget.

I always try to identify some probable good outcomes from the outset of any story. I mentally place those good outcomes in act five straight away, especially if a path seems to be a long and challenging one. Therefore, I always fully understand why I am walking this path and what things I may expect at the end.

When it comes to this specific story, I was able to identify three main constructive elements at the outset.

- *Personal growth* – I thought that I had learned a lot of things from the research I did for this book and managed to grow as a person to make it possible.
- *Self-actualisation* – I was very glad that by deciding to write this book I wasn't afraid to seek self-actualisation and fulfil part of my creative potential.
- *Helping others* – I hoped that some of the thoughts and ideas expressed in this book might prove useful at least for some people. If so, this journey was definitely worthwhile.

Whenever I felt down, whenever I was having recurring doubts about the importance of this work, especially in acts two and three, I always reminded myself about those three constructive outcomes at the end. Once I thought about them, I always felt empowered to continue my quest, no matter what.

STORY #2:
The battle for Kyiv

It is a fantastic experience when you can plan your story and actually live it as you wanted. Maybe you can close your eyes and see yourself on holiday next year. Maybe you can picture yourself starting your own business and the future success that follows. Maybe you have even mapped out the next twenty years of your life. Perhaps you have it all figured out: college, work, marriage, children, business, travel, retirement.

Having a good plan is important, without doubt. It is something that helps us to build the future we want. But it is also important to remember that life does not always go according to plan. There is a chance that at some point in your life you may be thrown into a story that you never wanted to live. It may be a scenario that was even impossible to imagine.

But we can still own a story, even it feels to be an imposed one. You can still be the author who shapes the narrative. You can still picture yourself as a protagonist who learns and grows during this period, even if you never wanted to take part in this particular script and go through such a difficult time. As such, you can stop feeling like a character in someone's else plot and continue consciously designing the life that you want to live.

Introduction: Planning my next chapter

It was the end of February 2022. I had just finished writing this book and had delivered it to the publisher, feeling exhausted but extremely happy that this long-term project was finally done. It was not even a week later. I was staying in Kyiv, visiting my family and friends and celebrating this big event. My calendar featured one event only: to link up with my publisher to discuss the design of the illustrations for this book. After that, I looked forward to planning a long-awaited holiday.

The big plan was to discover some new surf spots and to spend a few months living far, far away, most probably somewhere in Asia. I imagined how I would grab my surfboard early in the morning and would head to the ocean, before it is too hot and when it is not very crowded. It is a joy just to be near the ocean and observe its beauty but riding waves and connecting with the ocean is a form of meditation for me and one of the best ways to recharge my batteries. I also thought that after my morning surf session I would take a bike and go along the coastline. I would eventually stop at some nice coffee house to have breakfast and rest a bit.

Then, most likely, I would open my laptop and do some light work on my mobile app (Brightway.app). If you did not know, I actually have two careers that I have been developing in parallel. One is connected to academia, psychology and writing. And the second is connected to IT, to the development of mobile and web apps, to be more exact. Brightway, for example, is a journaling app. I was developing it as a tool to help people to record their daily life and create a happier and healthier mind.

Anyway, back then I wanted to design a few new features for the application and I thought that I would work on them between my surfing sessions. Yes, I know it is a holiday time, but this kind of creative work brings me joy even on holiday.

In sum, that's a brief overview of how I planned to live the first half of 2022. As a matter of fact, that's how I mapped out my next life chapter, my next story. But none of this was meant to happen. As someone said once: 'If you want to make God laugh, tell him about your plans.' On 24 February 2022, just like millions of other people, I woke up to sounds of bombing deep in the night.

Act one: The invasion

Overnight, on 24 February 2022, Russia launched a full-blown invasion of Ukraine after months of a build-up on Ukraine's border. Russia's president, Vladimir Putin, characterised it as a 'special military operation' to 'demilitarise and denazify' Ukraine. Nobody understood what this meant at that time. But what followed was the largest ground war in Europe since the Second World War, with numerous war crimes being committed in the process.

It all began in the early hours of the morning. Bombs fell on military facilities. Missiles and shelling struck several Ukrainian cities, including the capital, Kyiv. Columns of Russian troops and tanks rolled across the borders from the north and landed in the south.

The next few weeks were like living in a fog. Nobody could believe what was happening: here are lines of cars stretching back for dozens of kilometres on highways trying to move out of the cities ... Here are hundreds of people lined up at ATMs and even longer queues to stock up on food and water ... Here I shelter two friends at my place during air raids ... Here we are glued to our phones for the latest news ... Here we are taping up windows hoping it will help against flying debris ... Here everyone is trying to figure out what to do next.

The situation got worse with every day. It was reported that missiles and bombs were raining down on Ukrainian cities. Airstrikes indiscriminately hit civilian sites, including residential buildings, hospitals, schools, theatres and shopping malls. Fire was opened on civilian cars while they were trying to leave the occupied territories.

What's worse, at the start of Russia's invasion, Putin publicly raised the possibility of a nuclear strike. At first, in a televised speech announcing the 'military operation' in Ukraine, he warned other countries that 'whoever tries to stop us' would face 'the consequences you have never seen in your history'. Later that week, Putin ordered his military command to put Russia's nuclear deterrent forces on high alert, raising fears that he might use weapons of mass destruction, whether by design or out of despair.

It all looked as if the worst nightmare was about to come true. On 4 March, around 4 a.m., I woke up and read the news about fierce battles for control of the Zaporizhzhia nuclear power plant. It was reported that fire had broken out at the plant after it was hit by Russian shelling.

I was horrified, more so than I had ever been before. My first urge was to phone my family and friends to warn them about the danger. But I quickly realised that it would not help. The Zaporizhzhia nuclear power plant is the largest nuclear facility in Europe. If there was an explosion, there would be no safe place. Such a contingency would endanger the whole European continent and render much of Ukraine uninhabitable for decades.

It was the breaking point for me. It felt that tomorrow there may not be the world that I loved so much. There may not be literally any place for life. There may not be any place for growth.

I was not able to fall asleep again that night. Later that morning, I got my bag from the wardrobe and started packing, not completely sure what kind of stuff to put in it. Soon after, I arrived at an army recruitment department to sign up for military service.

Act two: The service

After the interview and assessment process, I was enlisted in the State Cyber Protection Centre, which was located in the capital, Kyiv. The decision was based on my background in IT and years of work abroad. Luckily, apart from self-care apps, I had also worked on projects that concerned cybersecurity.

The centre was formed to participate in cyber defence activities. There were top-notch specialists who identified and neutralised cyber attacks on the public and government sector. The goal was to ensure that people could stay safe and secure online. It was especially pressing during the war when the number of targeted hacking attacks skyrocketed.

But it was only part of the problem. At the start of the war, the Russian army was also targeting Ukraine's communications and internet infrastructure. For example, on 1 March, a Russian missile hit the Kyiv TV tower, killing five people and taking dozens of channels off air for a while. Such strikes were meant to disrupt communications and cut off the country from the internet and national media. Basically, if the attacks were successful, people would not be able to call loved ones, find out the latest news or access internet services.

I was enlisted in a combat unit at the centre. There was nothing we could do about airstrikes on our buildings, but we could guard some key infrastructure targets and thwart Russian sabotage operations inside the city.

By that time, Russian sabotage groups had snaked their way through the front lines and infiltrated the city. These groups might take over government buildings, lay mines, mark targets for Russian artillery, place hidden cameras, attack military checkpoints or assassinate leading politicians. Saboteurs were normally dressed in ordinary clothes. But they were also known to disguise themselves sometimes as the Ukrainian army or police officers. So sometimes it was really hard to tell who was who.

Our unit was primarily responsible for the safety of the centre, which was one of the bastions of cyber defence in the country. We took on the task of defending the building, all its technologies and people, during the attack on Kyiv. On top of that, we were helping other military units to patrol a local district to spot and capture sabotage groups.

The first days on duty were a trying experience. I was getting used to the weight of my plate carrier and the uncomfortable feeling of holding a gun in my hands. A senior officer showed me around and explained the duties of our team in the coming days.

I guess it would have been like an ordinary day had it not been interrupted by a droning sound overhead. The team glanced up to the sky to see where it was coming from. A second later, a powerful explosion rocked the street. Everyone instantly fell to the ground and scrambled to seek shelter.

In cases like this, everything happens so quickly that you don't think what to do. You just react. After that, you are overcome with a cocktail of conflicting feelings. There is both the experience of adrenaline and horror. There is joy that you are still alive. There is even curiosity that mixes with the keen sense of present danger. Many eyewitnesses take videos of the destruction and even go to the site of the explosions, which is a really bad idea.

That day, it turned out that Ukrainian air defence forces stepped in and intercepted an incoming ballistic missile over our positions. The missile was shot down around 150 metres above our heads. The shockwave from the blast shattered the windows of apartment buildings. The remnants of the intercepted missile fell in separate areas across the street. I don't know whether the missile was targeting exactly our positions or other facilities nearby. I was just happy that, luckily, nobody was hurt in that attack.

It was a completely new world, unknown to me. An overnight curfew was set to begin each day from 10 p.m. till 6 a.m. It was strictly forbidden to be outside during those hours. Those who were in the streets without a special pass were considered to be potential members of the enemy's reconnaissance and sabotage groups.

By the second week of the war, Kyiv had turned into a

fortress. Makeshift checkpoints were erected around the city, with blue-and-yellow national flags flying above them. Concrete blocks, anti-tank hedgehogs, mounds of sandbags and giant truck tyres topped with sand could be seen on almost every street. All of them were used as barriers to slow the advance of enemy troops down the city streets.

On 10 March, it was reported that nearly 2 million people, around half the population of Kyiv, had fled the city since the start of the war. The streets that were usually full of life and energy were now empty. There were lonely passers-by walking along deserted streets. Occasional cars appeared on the horizon. Those residents who stayed hid indoors or sought safety in bomb shelters. Tens of thousands of people crammed into every corner of subway stations or underground parking garages to shelter from airstrikes shaking the ground above them.

After a while, I started to recognise the faces of people who lived in the neighbourhood. Every morning, around 6 a.m., there was a mother with a little daughter who were returning home holding hands after spending a night in a bomb shelter that was located across the street. Soon after them, there was an elderly couple who were returning to the same apartment building carrying a small bag that looked like an emergency kit.

Act three: The siege
Each night in those early days of the war felt more sinister than the previous one. A huge convoy of Russian armoured vehicles, which stretched for about 64 kilometres (40 miles), was heading towards Kyiv from the north. Russian forces

were advancing, capturing several towns on their way. Fierce fighting was taking place in the outskirts of Kyiv.

The explosions grew louder, creeping closer to the city centre. After a while, you begin to notice the difference between these explosions and can distinguish between the artillery firing, air defence shooting or bombardment. But at first you walk with wide eyes open and you keep asking experienced soldiers: 'What was that?'

The piercing sound of air-raid sirens became a new daily norm. At night, you could see how huge explosions lit up the sky and echoed through the darkness. As daylight broke, clouds of smoke could be seen swirling up into the air. From time to time, bursts of gunfire rattled out across the city. Sometimes it all looked like a picture from an apocalypse movie.

Yet, amid war and brutality, there was also a place for love and kindness. Those who stayed in the neighbourhood bonded. People became closer. Even though everyone was gripped by fear, most people were friendly. Everyone tried to help. Some volunteers sewed bulletproof vests. Men brought wood so that the patrols could warm up by the fire burning in iron barrels during long freezing nights. Many women volunteered to cook and brought food for the military, elderly, hospitals, or anyone who was in need.

There was an old man with a big moustache, a former military man, who brought tea twice a day to our checkpoint. He always asked whether everyone was all right and then stood with us for a while discussing the latest news. We were all together during those days, probably as never before.

One night, we saw a stray dog running around our

position. It was a female, mid-size, with white fur. She looked dazed and disoriented because of the bursts of gunfire and blasts nearby. She would not eat the offered food, even though she was very skinny. The pup did not understand what was happening. She had shut down and just kept staring in the direction of where all the hellish sounds were coming from, while her back legs were slightly shaking.

It was a heartbreaking picture. I wanted to spend some time with her and create a cosy, safe environment. I felt really sorry that she had to go through all of this. I started slowly to pat her back and tell her with a calm, soft voice that everything's gonna be okay. 'You are gorgeous, you know that?' 'You are safe now.'

I told her about the guys in our team – where they came from and what they had been doing in their past lives. For example, the tallest guy in the team, named Ruslan, was a lawyer and used to work in a big IT company before the war. Further away, the biggest guy drinking tea had always been a military man and used to serve in the special forces, but she should not worry because even though he looked like a bear, he was the kindest soul and would give her a lot of hugs.

I was complaining that I had to watch a very dark area that night that was connected to a construction site that did not have illumination at all. But she should not worry, again, as we had already developed good night vision during the last couple of weeks, pretty much as owls had, so we would spot any danger quickly and protect her.

Soon, the whole team was giving the doggy 'touch therapy'. A few hours later, the pup had calmed down a little bit and even ate some sausage from one of our sandwiches.

When we were moving to other positions early in the morning, she walked with us and would not leave. She sneaked into a coffee house where we were storing some of our weapons and lay down among the boxes of anti-tank rockets, with big eyes full of fear and hope at the same time. It was decided: from now on, we had a new team member. We called her Grace.

On 22 March, the Ukrainian army mounted a counteroffensive to push Russian forces out of the Kyiv region. Soon, the Ukrainian forces made progress and reclaimed a series of towns.

Act four: Self-care

Honestly, self-care was not something that I paid much attention to during the first weeks of the war. You just try to survive and protect the people around you. That's the only priority.

I returned to my self-care practice basically only when I adapted a bit to the new conditions of life. Plus, there were some disturbing symptoms that I could not ignore any more.

First, I started to feel that there were some changes in my perception or in my tracking of time. Sometimes it felt that it was just one, horrible, long day. Partly, this can be explained by the military routine. Roughly speaking, you do the same thing every day. You wake up, you eat, you go on duty, and then sleep. And then the cycle repeats. You have no weekends, no breaks. You just live the same day over and over again. It feels pretty much like a military *Groundhog Day*. What makes matters worse is that we went on duty both during the day and at night. So there was no usual understanding that you could work in the daytime and then rest at night.

Second, I noticed that there was something weird going on with people's memory. The most common symptom was that many people sometimes had a hard time retrieving information from their long-term memory, even well-known facts. A few times I recognised that it took me, too, longer to recall some specific information than usual. The most obvious explanation in this case was stress and sleep deprivation. When a person is under acute stress or doesn't have enough sleep-hours to rest, they may have more difficulty recalling information or forming new memories.

In essence, the main tool for me to practise self-care during this time was journaling. All I had to do was to jot a few things down from time to time. That's it.

First and foremost, journaling is a great stress-management tool. Whenever there was a need, I wrote down my emotions and thoughts related to stressful events that happened throughout the day. It was useful to unravel whatever was entangled inside me, to release my emotional tension, and to address any worries.

In addition, journaling was great for keeping track of my life. Every day, I tried to record a few things that happened, such as notable events, memorable moments, or any activities. It is known as keeping a daily log. The easiest way to do this exercise is to write down three things that happened during the day. Before I did this, it felt that the days were blending into each other. But when I started making a daily summary of each day, it became much easier for me to separate one day from the next and to restore the normal sense of time. Plus, by writing things down, I could remember important events in greater detail and with more accuracy later on.

This kind of self-care was not very difficult for me. Journaling was a part of my daily routine before the war, not to mention my regular work on my own journal app. So, all I had to do was to return to this old good habit.

Act five: The victory

Russian efforts to occupy Kyiv ultimately came to naught. Following a series of successful Ukrainian counterattacks, on 29 March it was announced that Russia was withdrawing its forces from the Kyiv region. On 2 April, the Ukrainian authorities declared that the entire Kyiv region had been liberated.

As time passed, Kyiv slowly recovered. Anti-tank obstacles were moved aside to unblock the streets. Public transport was up and running again. The empty shelves in supermarkets were restocked. Cafés, restaurants, markets and barbershops were reopening and welcoming visitors again.

More and more cars and people could be seen in the streets. Families that had left the city in the opening days of the war were gradually returning to their homes. There was still a continued threat of Russian airstrikes, and air-raid sirens blared across the city almost every day. But it looked like the city was getting back to something resembling normal life.

On one April day, I was strolling around a district that we used to patrol. Life was noticeably returning to its streets. I saw the faces that had become so familiar during the last month. The members of our team were drinking coffee at a coffee house that had recently reopened. There was Grace, wearing a new blue collar. She looked so much better now, with a smile on her face and constantly wagging her tail. It even seemed that she had gained a lot more weight, as she looked much fluffier now. There was the old man with the big moustache who was laughing and chit-chatting with the military. The woman and the little girl who used to hide in the bomb shelter were now walking peacefully down the street.

I saw everyone alive. They were smiling and doing ordinary things, which we all take for granted in everyday life, but which we also missed so much during the siege. It was probably the first time I had felt real happiness in the last couple of months.

At times, I returned to the reflections that I had had a long time ago, during my undergrad years, and which drove me to study psychology and write this book. I imagined: *What if those great rulers of the past and present had 'started with themselves'? What if they knew how to identify and challenge their biases? What if they didn't take their anger and hurt out on others? What if they were at peace with themselves? Maybe, in such scenarios, there would be less wars and violence in this world?*

I then felt a wave of sorrow and acute pain in almost every part of my body. I felt devastated that in our modern times, there were still too many individuals who would resort to savagery. I felt sad that there were lots of people who supported and justified wars. I felt heartbroken that too many were suffering and being killed right now, and I couldn't stop this madness.

But among the thoughts that were running through my mind, there was one that was giving me at least some comfort: *I could still start with myself.* It was something that it was still possible to control. I could try not to forget to take care of my mental health. I could continue working on my personal development. By doing that, I could cultivate inner peace. I could maintain peace of mind.

Of course, I wouldn't be able to stop any wars or cruelty on the planet. But I know that when I live at peace with myself, I want to maintain peace and harmony around myself. In my family, in the circle of my friends, at work, in my neighbourhood.

Maybe sometimes I could comfort those who feel scared. Maybe I will have enough strength to defend those who need protection. Maybe I could help to fix what was broken or build even more beautiful things. Perhaps it won't change the whole world. *But that's a good beginning*, I thought again.

12

The Pyramid Master

THE TRANSITION GAME

If a person learns, for example, boxing, karate and wrestling, it does not automatically mean that they train in MMA. It only means that they train in multiple styles separately. What one does not necessarily know in this case is how to combine those styles into one cohesive whole.

When you train in MMA, however, you learn how to merge different styles into one. An athlete knows when to put various moves together, making seamless transitions between stand-up striking, clinching and grappling on the ground.

Now, let's assume you've mastered a number of self-care techniques. What comes next? The next step is to learn how to work on multiple levels in sequence. The idea is not to develop your skills entirely in isolation, but gradually learn to weave those threads together (in a way that contributes to an overall goal of self-care and personal development).

Ultimately, you will learn to work on all six levels of the Pyramid Model, from the top to the bottom, and your inner journey might look something like the following:

STEP #1:
Stay well

Sometimes you may feel like you are
sleepwalking through life. There is this
sense of things being dull, repetitive,
predictable. Days fly by, as do the weeks,
months and years. As we rush through life,
it is very easy to stop noticing the novelty
and the beauty of the world around us.

Think about it this way. Awareness is like
a source of light illuminating your way.
Every day, the sun rises and gives us light,
warmth and growth to plants. Similarly,
every single day, as you wake up, there is

a possibility that your awareness will rise
high and shine bright, giving you a sense
of clarity, inner warmth and growth.

Whatever your goals are, just remind
yourself to start each of your journeys
awake and aware of the present moment.
And as you move on, don't forget to keep
the sun of your awareness shining. Wake
up in each moment, again and again.

STEP #2:
Think well

Once you have embarked on a journey,
sometimes you may find yourself getting
lost. There are many road signs that point
in different directions. There are lots of
dangerous paths, about which we don't
know anything. If we end up in the wrong
place, we may have an urge to panic and
run, which may get us only more lost.

Imagine that the belief system is like your
inner navigation tool. Your goals and values
are a sort of map that shows you where you
want to go. Meanwhile, your ability to think
clearly and realistically is like a compass

that indicates the course and direction. If you know how to use this tool, you will be always clear about your co-ordinates.

So, when you come to a fork next time, you will always know where you are going and which direction is right for you.

STEP #3:
Remember well

The path to our goals is rarely a straight
line. There are almost always obstacles,
traps or challenges on the way. There may
be bandits on the road who want to rob or
hurt you; contingencies may slow you down.
You may also mess up sometimes or fail at
what you're doing, no matter how smart or
lucky you are, since nobody is perfect.

Think of memories as plants in your own
garden. Good memories are like flowers;
just looking at them can make you smile.

Bad memories are more like trees. It takes
longer for a tree to grow. But with time,

it can give you fruits, air to breath, and shade to hide in on a hot day. By the same token, many rough experiences can prove to be very useful at some point, though it usually takes a while for us to see that.

But one day, just as you can pluck fruit from a tree, you may discover that you can take a lesson from a past negative experience – a lesson that will feed you, make you a little bit stronger and help you continue your quest.

In addition, just as you can sit in the shade of a tree on a hot day to cool down, you may discover that you can find some comfort and peace reflecting on your past negative experiences, understanding how far you actually went and how resilient and wise you have become since that time.

Just don't forget that you can intentionally take care of flowers and trees as you move forward, keeping your path lush and blooming.

STEP #4:
Feel well

When we go through a rough time or
experience a setback, it is very easy to
feel stressed out. When feeling emotional
overwhelm, you may act without thinking,
snap at others, or end up doing things you'll
later regret. You may also forget all that spark
of joy, passion and fulfilment that you felt
when you embarked on your journey.

In some sense, our emotional nature is
akin to fire. Both emotions and fire are
necessary for our survival. But if not kept
in check, they can cause a lot of trouble.

For example, if left unattended, the flames of a camp-fire can inadvertently get out of control, setting your tent or the ground ablaze. But when you know how to manage the flames, you can stay warm, cook meals and create a cosy atmosphere that will attract other travellers.

Similarly, if left unattended, our emotions can spin out of control and turn into an inferno, burning down everything in their way. But if you develop the skills to manage your feelings, it is likely that you will know how to cope with the stresses of everyday life, how to bring calm to yourself or a situation, and how to stay positive despite the circumstances. And even if the colder weather comes around, the kindness of your heart may still keep you and other travellers a little bit warmer.

Just don't forget to ask yourself once in a while: 'How am I feeling now?' This way, you will always know when it is time to camp during a hard day and recharge a bit.

If done regularly, the next morning, soon after waking up, you will always have a drive to continue your quest, acting with grace and inner calm, without resorting to brutal force, even in stressful situations.

STEP #5:
Speak well

On days when things don't go exactly as
planned, when we are beset by intense
emotions, it is very easy to start misusing our
words. You may want to blame others for your
difficulties or misfortunes. Or you may be
prompted to berate yourself for every failure or
wrong decision ever made during your journey.

I am not saying that you can't speak
negatively sometimes, if you want to. I
am just saying that we should not forget
to say constructive things after that.

330

Though you can't control everything that happens on your path, you can control how you write your travel journal. You can make sure that there is always something good in each of your stories. You can make sure that your protagonist (a.k.a. you) gets better with every new chapter.

It won't take long for such stories to build you up. And perhaps your words will also inspire those you meet along the way.

STEP #6:
Act well

Any journey takes time and effort. After a
day or month of walking, sooner or later
you will get fatigued, no matter how strong
you are. You may just collapse and fall to
the ground, being completely exhausted and
unable to move for weeks. Or at one point,
you may just feel an urge to turn back, as
the path now seems to be too difficult.

The trick is not to try to run a thousand miles all
at one time. It is not about pushing harder. It will
only make you stressed and worn out very quickly.

The trick is to take small and consistent
steps every day, which will eventually
lead you to your destination.

332

Part Four

Visual summary

Appendix

How to Develop
Advanced Skills

Want to dive deeper and learn more about how to develop yourself personally? Here are the next steps that you can take:

1. Download the app
Download the Brightway journaling app to have a training tool for everyday practice. The app allows you to do digitally most of the exercises discussed in *The Pyramid Mind*, and it contains additional learning resources, which makes it a perfect companion to your practice. You can download the app free from the App Store or Google Play, or learn more at: www.brightway.app

2. Learn from the course
Take my online course to deepen your knowledge and get advanced training. The course shares more strategies and teaches you how to develop the skills of personal mastery in a clear and easy-to-follow format, through video lessons.

Learn more at: vladbeliavsky.com/courses

3. Subscribe to the newsletter

Get additional helpful content sent straight to your inbox. Approximately once a month, I send a newsletter with new ideas about psychology, motivational content or practical tips for self-care. You will be also the first to hear about my newest books and projects.

You can sign up at: vladbeliavsky.com/newsletter

4. Join the community

The final step is to join a community to have more support during your journey. Of course, we can walk alone on our journey of personal growth. But it is an incredible joy to meet like-minded people who share your values, who may become your friends, and who can give you a hand on your path.

Building a community is something new to me, to be honest. Being a fairly introverted guy, I used to walk on my own. But I do believe that we can achieve a positive change much faster if we walk together.

If you have the passion for personal mastery, want to 'start with yourself' and still want to make the surrounding world a better place, I warmly invite you to join our small but growing international community of fantastic people.

You can join the community on Instagram. Follow: @vlad.beliavsky or @brightway.app

How to Use the App

In the middle of writing this book, I asked myself: 'How can I make the self-care practice for my readers easier?' The exercises described in this book are not very difficult themselves, but to do most of them you will need a pen and some paper. Having a personal notebook to do exercises is the proven and common approach which is often used during actual therapy sessions. I call it the old-school style. And it can certainly work for you.

Yet it also has its own drawbacks. One of them is that it is hard to make edits to your notes. If you make a mistake, or want to correct what you've written, or want to add more text to a specific page, it is always hard to do this in a physical notebook. You need to cross it out, write it again, or even start from the very beginning. That's what has always annoyed me.

I really wanted to make your (and my) practice much easier and more effective. That's why I started the development of a mobile app, which would be a powerful training tool and a companion to your practice. That's how Brightway was born.

ABOUT BRIGHTWAY

At its core, Brightway is a journaling app. As with any other journaling app, it can be used to record your life journey for personal or professional use. But Brightway is also a self-care app that is based on the principles of integrative psychology to create a healthier and happier mind. In fact, it was designed specifically to help you work on all levels of your mind. Here is a short overview of each level:

Mind level	App exercise
Reason	Journaling is one of the easiest ways to incorporate mindfulness into your life. By making regular journal notes, you become more aware of what you think, feel and what is going on in your life.
Thoughts	You can use the journal to clear your mind, keep a record of your thoughts, set your goals or self-reflect. To make it easier, Brightway has default templates that will help you to identify and challenge your negative thoughts.
Memories	Keeping a journal is arguably the best tool for recording your life and making sure you won't forget any precious moment. In addition to that, Brightway has a guided framework to do monthly and annual reviews, which allow you to reflect on a particular area of your life, to get insight and learn from past experiences.
Emotions	Writing helps to express any difficult feelings in a private and secure space, reduce stress, practise gratitude or to track your mood over a period of time.

Mind level	App exercise
Words	You can keep a journal to create stories about important periods of your life. To simplify this exercise, Brightway has default templates with prompts and building blocks that will guide you to create constructive stories.
Behaviour	Finally, you can use the journal to track your routines, make notes on how to improve certain behaviours, or log your progress.

In addition, there are also video lessons and educational materials that will coach and guide you in your practice.

Learn more at: **Download for free:**

Website: brightway.app   Available both at the App
Instagram: brightway.app   Store and Google Play

How to Apply These Ideas to Business

I am occasionally asked to speak at Fortune 500 companies and organisations around the world about how to apply the science of how our mind works to help to build more effective teams, corporate cultures and businesses. I've put together some of the most practical tips in a short bonus chapter.

You can download this chapter at:
https://vladbeliavsky.com/business

Acknowledgements

Before anyone else, I must thank my family, not only for their support and encouragement on this book but also for letting me pursue my goals and standing by me during every success and struggle. Without them, this project may not exist at all. I want to let my mum, dad, brother and sister know that I love them.

Second, I am grateful to my agent, Rachel Mills, for believing in this project in the first place, for reading early drafts, for her patience, optimism and guidance at every step of the publishing process.

Third, I owe a debt of gratitude to my editors, Kaiya Shang and Alison Macdonald, for helping to make this book a reality. Kaiya gave me the freedom and trust to create a book I am really proud of and showed incredible support at various stages of writing. Alison, with her experience and skill set, did a great job to bring this project to a successful end.

Of course, to the whole team at Simon & Schuster, who helped with editing, designing and marketing – thank you.

Special thanks to my development team, who kept working on our tech projects and the Brightway app when I was in the military.

Of course, I am indebted to those people with whom I

served during the Russian invasion of Ukraine in 2022 – who were defending their homeland and covering my back (while I still had to call my publisher occasionally to prepare the book for release). Special thanks to Sergiy Kruglyk for being a good friend and brother-in-arms.

Many thanks to all my friends, family and colleagues who ever asked 'How's your book?' and offered a word of encouragement. It is always a pleasure to know that there are people who are genuinely interested in your work. But it is a relief to hear a kind word when you get stuck and struggle with writing at some point.

And, of course, to you, my dear reader. Thank you so much for taking the time to read this book and joining me on this journey. This is a book that is very personal to me. With all the research, writing and challenges on the way – like looking for the right agent and publisher, the global pandemic and war – it took me around a decade to complete it. And knowing that there are people who have read your book till the very end is definitely a rewarding experience. So, thank you, my dear reader!

– October 2022

Notes

In this section, I have included a list of references, additional notes and suggested reading. I expect that most readers will find this list sufficient and helpful. But I realise that this bibliography may not be exhaustive, as the format of this book differs from a common academic manuscript. If you notice that I did not give credit to someone or made a mistake somewhere in the book, please email me at vladbeliavsky.com/contact, and I will try to make amendments as soon as possible.

Introduction

More on integrative psychotherapy:

Norcross, J. C. and Goldfried, M. R. (eds.), *Handbook of Psychotherapy Integration* (3rd ed.), Oxford University Press (2019). https://doi.org/10.1093/med-psych/9780190690465.001.0001

Research on the number of counsellors in Britain who use the integrative approach:

Hollanders, H. and McLeod, J. 'Theoretical orientation and reported practice: A survey of eclecticism among counsellors in Britain', *British Journal of Guidance and Counselling*, 27(3), 405–414 (1999). https://doi.org/10.1080/03069889908256280

More on philosophical questions, issues and the integrative approach:

Beliavsky, V., *'Freedom, Responsibility, and Therapy'*, Palgrave Macmillan (2020). https://link.springer.com/book/10.1007/978-3-030-41571-6

More on the trends and future of psychotherapy:

Norcross, J. C., Pfund, R. A. and Cook, D. M., 'The predicted future of psychotherapy: A decennial e-Delphi poll', *Professional Psychology: Research and Practice*, 53(2), 109–115 (2022). https://doi.org/10.1037/pro0000431

Chapter 2

More on memory systems:

Squire, L. R. and Dede, A. J., 'Conscious and unconscious memory systems', *Cold Spring Harbor Perspectives in Biology*, 7(3), a021667 (2015). https://doi.org/10.1101/cshperspect.a021667

More on episodic memory:

The term 'episodic memory' was first coined in 1972 by Endel Tulving to describe the difference between 'remembering' and 'knowing'. Tulving, E., 'Episodic memory: From mind to brain', *Annual Review of Psychology*, 53, 1–25 (2002).

More on emotional memory:

LeDoux, J., *The Emotional Brain: The Mysterious Underpinnings of Emotional Life*, Simon & Schuster (1998).

Phelps, E. A., 'Human emotion and memory: interactions of the amygdala and hippocampal complex', *Current Opinion in Neurobiology*, 14(2), 198–202 (2004). https://doi.org/10.1016/j.conb.2004.03.015

More on the role of procedural memory in speech:

Ullman, M. T., 'A neurocognitive perspective on language: the declarative/procedural model', *Nature Reviews Neuroscience*, 2, 717–726 (2001). doi: 10.1038/35094573

Chapter 3

More on memory disfunction:

Matthews, B. R., 'Memory dysfunction', *Continuum*, 21(3), 613–26 (2015). https://www.ncbi.nlm.nih.gov/pmc/articles/PMC4455839/

Budson, A. E. and Price, B. H., 'Memory dysfunction', *New England Journal of Medicine*, 352(7), 692–699 (2005). https://doi.org/10.1056/NEJMra041071

More on disorders of language and their relation to procedural memory:

Ullman, M. T., Earle, F. S., Walenski, M. and Janacsek, K., 'The neurocognition of developmental disorders of language', *Annual Review of Psychology*, 71, 389–417 (2020). doi: 10.1146/annurev-psych-122216-011555

More on H. M. patient:

Corkin, S., *Permanent Present Tense: The Unforgettable Life of the Amnesic Patient, H. M.*, Basic Books (2013).

More on the story reported by Claparède:

LeDoux, J., *The Emotional Brain: The Mysterious Underpinnings of Emotional Life*, Simon & Schuster (1998).

The experiment by researchers from the University of Iowa on emotional memory:

Bechara, A., Tranel, D., Damasio, H., Adolphs, R., Rockland, C. and Damasio, A. R., 'Double dissociation of conditioning and declarative knowledge relative to the amygdala and hippocampus in humans', *Science*, 269(5227), 1115–18 (1995). https://pubmed.ncbi.nlm.nih.gov/7652558/

Michael Johnson's interview:

https://olympics.com/en/news/
michael-johnson-stroke-recovery-awareness-campaign

Michael Phelps's interview:

https://people.com/sports/michael-phelps-opens-up-about-adhd-
struggles-in-new-video-a-teacher-told-me-id-never-amount-to-
anything/

Chapter 5

On a definition of mindfulness:

Bishop, S. R., Lau, M., Shapiro, S., Carlson, L., Anderson, N. D.,
Carmody, J., Segal, Z. V., Abbey, S., Speca, M., Velting, D, and
Devins, G., 'Mindfulness: a proposed operational definition',
Clinical Psychology: Science and Practice, 11(3), 230–41 (2004).
https://www.personal.kent.edu/~dfresco/mindfulness/
Bishop_et_al.pdf

More on mindfulness:

Kabat-Zinn, J., *Wherever You Go, There You Are: Mindfulness
Meditation in Everyday Life*, Hachette Books (2010).

Chapter 6

Research on optimists, pessimists and realists, and longterm mental health:

de Meza, D. and Dawson, C., 'Neither an optimist nor a
pessimist be: mistaken expectations lower wellbeing' *Personality
and Social Psychology bulletin*, 47(4), 540–550 (2021). https://doi.
org/10.1177/0146167220934577

More on CBT and its techniques:

Beck, J. S., *Cognitive Behavior Therapy: Basics and Beyond* (3rd
edn), Guilford Press (2020).

Chapter 7

More on rumination:

Sansone, R. A. and Sansone, L. A., 'Rumination: Relationships with physical health', *Innovations in Clinical Neuroscience*, 9(2), 29–34 (2012). https://www.ncbi.nlm.nih.gov/pmc/articles/PMC3312901/

Research on the third-person perspective:

Kross, E. and Ayduk, O., 'Self-distancing: Theory, research, and current directions', in Olson, J. M. and Zanna, M. P. (eds), *Advances in Experimental Social Psychology*, 55: 81–136 (2017).

Wallace-Hadrill, S. M. and Kamboj, S. K., 'The impact of perspective change as a cognitive reappraisal strategy on affect: a systematic review', *Frontiers in Psychology*, 7(1715) (2016). https://doi.org/10.3389/fpsyg.2016.01715

On different ways of reminiscing:

Wong, P. T. and Watt, L. M., 'What types of reminiscence are associated with successful aging?', *Psychology and Aging*, 6(2), 272–279 (1991).

Cappeliez, P. and O'Rourke, N., 'Profiles of reminiscence among older adults: perceived stress, life attitudes, and personality variables', *International Journal of Aging and Human Development*, 54(4), 255–66 (2002). doi: 10.2190/YKYB-K1DJ-D1VL-6M7W

Chapter 8

Research on categories of emotions:

Cowen, A.S. and Keltner D., 'Self-report captures 27 distinct categories of emotion bridged by continuous gradients', *PNAS*, (2017). doi: 10.1073/pnas.1702247114

Research on emotional labelling:

Lieberman, M. D., Eisenberger, N. I., Crockett, M. J., Tom, S. M., Pfeifer, J. H. and Way, B. M., 'Putting feelings into words: affect abelling disrupts amygdala activity in response to affective stimuli', *Psychological Science*, 18(5), 421–428 (2007). https://www.scn.ucla.edu/pdf/AL(2007).pdf

The experiment on exposure to a spider:

Kircanski, K., Lieberman, M. D. and Craske, M. G., 'Feelings into words: contributions of language to exposure therapy', *Psychological Science*, 23(10), 1086–91 (2012). https://journals.sagepub.com/doi/10.1177/0956797612443830

Chapter 9

On contamination stories:

McAdams, D. P., Reynolds, J. P., Lewis, M., Patten, A. H. and Bowman, P. J., 'When bad things turn good and good things turn bad: sequences of redemption and contamination in life narrative and their relation to psychosocial adaptation in midlife adults and in students', *Personality and Social Psychology Bulletin*, 27, 474–485 (2001).

The study that examined divorce rates based on oral interviews:

Buehlman, K. T., Gottman, J. M. and Katz, L. Y., 'How a couple views their past predicts their future: predicting divorce from an oral history interview', *Journal of Family Psychology*, 5, 295–318 (1992).

More on redemptive and competence-building stories:

Jones, B. K., Destin, M. and McAdams, D. P., 'Telling better stories: competence-building narrative themes increase adolescent persistence and academic achievement', *Journal of Experimental Social Psychology*, 76, 76–80 (2018).

More on how to work with our life stories:

Schneiderman, K., *Step Out of Your Story: Writing Exercises to Reframe and Transform Your Life*, New World Library (2015).

Chapter 10

Research on habits by Duke University, Durham, North Carolina:

Neal, David T., Wood, W., & Quinn, J. M., 'Habits: a repeat performance', *Current Directions in Psychological Science*, 15, 198–202 (2006).

Resarch on habit formation by UCL:

Lally, P., van Jaarsveld, C. H. M., Potts, H. W. W. and Wardle, J., 'How are habits formed: modelling habit formation in the real world', *European Journal of Social Psychology*, 40(6), 998–1009 (2010). https://doi.org/10.1002/ejsp.674

More on building habits:

Duhigg, C., *The Power of Habit: Why We Do What We Do in Life and Business*, Random House (2012).

Fogg, B. J., *Tiny Habits: The Small Changes That Change Everything*, Virgin Books (2020).

Index

ABOUT THE AUTHOR

Vlad Beliavsky PhD is a psychologist, philosopher and author. His research focuses on mental health, the functioning of the human mind, and how to improve performance and personality. Vlad specialises in integrative psychotherapy and developed a self-care method known as The Pyramid Model, which is presented for the general audience for the first time in *The Pyramid Mind*. He is also the founder and CEO of Brightway, a journal app which is designed to develop a healthier and happier mind.

With the start of the Russian invasion of Ukraine in 2022, Vlad enlisted in the Ukrainian Army, where he served in cyber defence and provided psychological support.

In peacetime, Vlad regularly works with organisations around the world, helping people to get the best out of themselves and build thriving cultures. Born in Ukraine and educated in the UK, Vlad normally splits his time between London and Kyiv.

Vlad holds a PhD in Philosophy from the University of Warwick, where he conducted research on psychotherapy and taught at the Department of Psychology.

Learn more at:
Website: vladbeliavsky.com
Instagram: @vlad.beliavsky
Facebook: @vlad.beliavsky
Twitter: @vlad_beliavsky
Mobile app: brightway.app